'*Is God Really Legit?* is a go[od] some of the big questions s[u] Neil's passion for the subject young people makes this [a] plenty of helpful follow-up resources.'
Hannah Malcolm, '*God and the Big Bang*' Coordinator
@GatBB_UK

'Easy to understand ... helped [me] understand that there might be a relationship with faith and science.'
Matt Vowles (aged 17)

'Too often teenagers are not allowed to ask questions; many worry that questioning God is not OK. This book gives young people the chance to seek answers and think outside the box. It does not have all the answers, but then who does? What a great way to get thinking about God and some of the big questions we all have about life. If you do not come away from this book with more questions than when you started it, you are not reading it right!'
Dr Lesley Gray, Secondary School Teacher and Science and Faith Communicator

Is God Really Legit?

Making Sense of Faith and Science

Neil Laing

instant
apostle

First published in Great Britain in 2018

Instant Apostle
The Barn
1 Watford House Lane
Watford
Herts
WD17 1BJ

British Library Cataloguing-in-Publication Data

A catalogue record for this book is available from the British Library

This book and all other Instant Apostle books are available from Instant Apostle:

Website: www.instantapostle.com
E-mail: info@instantapostle.com

ISBN 978-1-909728-83-7

Printed in Great Britain

Contents

Thanks

I owe a lot to so many people I couldn't begin to name them all. My parents, teachers, university lecturers, teachers at Bible college, various pastors over the years and friends and colleagues. I even owe a lot to people who disagree with me. Their challenge has helped me to understand issues. Although I disagree with Richard Dawkins, his book *The God Delusion* made me think (never a bad thing) and I came to understand better how radical atheists, like he is, reason things out. He emphasised the importance of evidence when looking at any issue, which is true. So, a thank you to him is due as well. Although some people think he has knock-down arguments against God, I reckon if that is the best an intelligent atheist can do, the weaknesses of his arguments convinced me even more that God is 'there'.

I do want to say a special thank you to Christina Biggs who runs Christians in Science in Bristol. She first challenged me to write my thoughts, and this produced my first book and led to this one. She has also been constantly encouraging as well as constructively critical as I've written them.

I also want to thank those people who have read this book and offered criticisms. I have asked a few teenagers to look at it. Quite a few agreed but never did so. Matt Vowles did. He offered some useful criticisms among his appreciations of the book in its last stages before its submission to the publishers. Thank you, Matt. One of my Year 11 ICT students who adores science, Meghann Wildman at The Castle School in Taunton, Somerset, read it in its first stages and gave me an extensive and helpful list of critiques and suggestions, reading it from a teenage viewpoint. Meghann, you're a champion!

I would also like to thank my publishers, Instant Apostle. Maybe you're thinking – 'Do you just add water and have an apostle?' Well, there was nothing instant about them. They went through the book really carefully and have given me loads of ace suggestions. This book would not be the same without them.

Finally, I would like especially to thank Hannah Malcolm of God and the Big Bang, an organisation that gives students from Years 6 to 13 (10–18-year-olds) an exciting opportunity to discover, discuss and debate the compatibility of science and faith. Hannah gave me some very useful suggestions for the book after reading an early version. She also supplied me with the Top Ten Questions Asked by Teenagers which were gleaned from considerable research done by God and the Big Bang collating the most common questions teenagers asked during their sessions. Thank you, Hannah. Your help has been invaluable.

Preface

A while ago, a lady called Christina Biggs, who leads a group in Bristol called Christians in Science, challenged me to read Professor Richard Dawkins' book, *The God Delusion*. You've probably heard of Dawkins. He's kind of like the atheist Rottweiler. Lots of people think he's just great; lots of others, even some atheists, think he's the opposite. Well, I have met him briefly and had a bit of email correspondence with him and he's been very friendly – he's an OK guy though he does seem to think anyone who disagrees with him is stupid. I'm sure he thinks I'm stupid!

Anyway, I read the book. I thought some of his arguments were quite good and some *seemed* to be good but were, to be honest, very weak. It's not that he's dim – he's very good on science, but he was out of his depth on some things – just as I am. He is highly qualified in biology and was educated at the University of Oxford (generally thought of as one of the world's very top universities). He's also a very good teacher – you would find his book quite easy to read. But his understanding of what Christians believe about God is sadly lacking.

Tina Biggs then challenged me to write a reply. She was thinking of something that would be suitable for some young people I had been taking to the Christians in Science meetings. I started to do it, but found it was difficult. So, I took the easy way out and wrote a book for adults. After all, Dawkins' book is aimed mainly at adults.

I wrote one called *Even Dawkins Has a God*. But I found that teenagers were asking for something for themselves so this one emerged slowly like a snail coming out of its shell.

I don't want to tell you what to believe; it must be your own belief. I want to give you things to think about; ways of arguing that will help you to think critically. The thing is this: lots of people will tell you God exists; loads of others will tell you He doesn't. What people think, what I think and even what you think will never be what decides whether He exists or not. What matters is the truth. It's not a democracy. We don't decide by a vote or debate if God is there. We don't decide based on how intelligent believers or unbelievers are.

If He isn't there, then it doesn't much matter what we think, as long as we don't do others harm. If He does exist, then it really does matter one massive amount. You are responsible for your life and for your response to Him if He is there. You can't blame God or anyone else if you get it wrong.

I'm not going to concentrate on Richard Dawkins' book and answer it because it's too long, but I will mention some things he says, as he speaks for a large group of atheists. You may find I challenge your beliefs (Christian or not). You never grow if you are afraid of having your beliefs challenged. You may end up with the same opinions you started with or you may change your mind about your beliefs. Both can be positive.

Bible versions

I am going to use two main Bible versions: The English Standard Version (ESV) and *The Message* Bible (MSG) which is a very modern paraphrase. I have also used the King James Version (KJV). In some cases, I have paraphrased the passage myself and sometimes, I have just referred to a verse without quoting it. In each case, I will give a reference and include the version (ESV, MSG or KJV) but if I have not actually quoted a verse or have paraphrased it, I won't give a version.

Now, all I ask of you before you start is that you have an open mind. I remember someone once telling me, 'A mind is a bit like a parachute – it doesn't work unless it's open!' So, please read on.

The Author's Story

I think it's important to know where someone is coming from when you read their books. Then you know what they believe and why they say what they do. If you were reading a political book and you knew the author was a Conservative, you would expect them to argue for Conservative politics and against socialist politics. It's important to know where I am coming from as well, so I thought I'd give you a potted history of how I came to what I believe now.

My upbringing was almost certainly very different from yours. My parents emigrated from the UK to Southern Rhodesia, now called Zimbabwe (my father in 1929 when he was only twenty-one and my mother just after the Second World War). I was born in the capital, Salisbury, now called Harare, and brought up on a farm to the  north. It had no electricity, and I still remember having our water delivered in large drums on the back of a Scotch cart pulled by two oxen. The water had been bucketed out of a stream coming out of the hills about four miles away.

When I was about three or four, we had a borehole drilled so we could pump our water out of an underground stream. The nearest village was twenty-five miles away and Salisbury (the nearest town) was ninety-six miles away. Our groceries were delivered on the back of a large lorry twice a week to the farm next door (four miles away) where we would collect it. When I was very small, the nearest doctor was seventy miles away, and in the rainy season[1] we would sometimes have to cross rivers in flood to get there. Basically, that meant you didn't cross till the water went down. Some cars got washed down rivers.

We had a very large garden and as children, my two brothers, my sister and I used to play in it all day. Occasionally, we had snakes such as cobras and puff adders coming into the house, which made life quite exciting! As we had cattle on the farm, sometimes we had leopards attacking the calves and my father had to shoot three leopards. We also once had hyenas killing cattle and, on one occasion, a male lion (with no mane) appeared. We had plenty of antelopes and so on, but it was always exciting to see them.

The nearest school was in the village, so my mother taught us using a correspondence course from the age of five and then at seven we went to boarding schools. My first one, for a year, was in the village. I hated it!

When my brother was old enough, we went together to a school about 280 miles away. We had to go into Salisbury and catch the overnight train to the eastern border town of Umtali (now Mutare) and then go by bus to the school in

---

[1] The rainy season in Zimbabwe is in the summer (November to March because it is in the southern hemisphere).

the Vumba Mountains nearby. It was called Eagle School[2] and I discovered that Richard Dawkins also went there a few years earlier than I did.

It was an excellent school but being that far from your parents at the age of eight was a bit much. I know all about homesickness! We had no half-terms – just twelve or thirteen weeks between holidays. My brother forgot what my parents looked like during his first term! I also found out what it was like to be bullied. I lost my temper quite easily, so the other boys took great delight in teasing me till I lashed out. But I wasn't much good at fighting anyway.

My parents were Christian believers. I wouldn't say they really understood much theology but they believed God existed, that Jesus was the Son of God and that they should live by a high moral code. That's what they taught us and that's how they lived. I remember my father once

[2] Image from http://www.swimhistory.org/champions/1900-1960/1956-olympics/item/422-rhodesia-schools-manicaland?start=2 (accessed 10th January 2015).

receiving one penny too much in change from a shop and discovering it well after he had left the store. So, he went back and returned it to the assistant!

We didn't make it to church 'services' that often as they were in the local village, but went more often than the majority of people in the district. My father was one of two people who built the church building. He was Presbyterian (Church of Scotland), coming from Scotland, and my mother, from England, was Anglican. We were all christened as Presbyterians. When we did go along, I must say, I found it deathly boring. It was always the same. My parents took it very seriously and thought you had to be incredibly quiet and reverent inside a church building. I got the impression God hated noise and fun.

My secondary school, Falcon College, was the other side of the country, about 390 miles away, and again we went by train and bus. It was almost military. We were caned for lack of effort in class, for having untidy beds and all sorts of other things. It certainly prepared me for the army later. At seventeen, I was confirmed, together with my brother Rob, at school, and I used to go regularly to Communion, thinking God must be very pleased with me. But it was still boring and I didn't think it related to real life much.

While I was there, I began keeping snakes (yes, poisonous ones) and hawks which I trained. The picture is of me with my second hawk (I've changed a bit since then). The school was on 2,000 acres and some of us spent all possible time out in the sticks, looking for eagles'

and hawks' nests. I kept records of birds' nesting habits and got really involved with wildlife. I decided I wanted to become a game ranger and go in for wildlife conservation.

So, after A levels, I did my Army National Service, then I worked for the Veterinary Research Department living in two huts (pictured) way out in the wild, shooting animals that were being removed from a corridor of land to try  to stop tsetse fly from spreading sleeping sickness to cattle. I had to collect parasites from the animals and take blood serum for research. This was for just a few months before going to university in Pietermaritzburg, South Africa, to study zoology and botany.

Unfortunately, I got very involved in karate at university. I captained the university team and reached 1st Dan Black Belt after two years. A couple of years later I reached 2nd Dan and captained a Rhodesian team in my style. That sounds great but it meant loads of training and I ended up mostly failing my second year and I left.

However, I knew, after my studies, that the idea of God suddenly creating everything 6,000 years ago was nonsense. I always took a Bible with me each term but never read it. I still believed there was a God because I didn't want to give up on my childhood acceptance, but I tried to reason it out and thought God was the sort of source of all physical laws and completely impersonal. I suppose I could only think of 'God' in terms of science. To be honest, I had really given up any genuine belief in God. I just didn't want to admit it.

After three years of going from one job to another, I knew I had to return and finish my degree. To fund it, I applied to do teaching and was accepted but first went to the UK for a year. It was there that I met my future wife, Lizzie. But I also started looking at where I was heading in life and wasn't all that thrilled with how I saw it panning out. You know: finish the degree, get married and have children, teach for forty years, retire, grow old and die. What a prospect! I sort of felt this hollow in my life. Something was missing but I hadn't a clue what.

When I returned to university, my old landlady kindly put me up in her flat while I looked for another place to live. While I was with her, she lent me a book called *Beyond Ourselves* by Catherine Marshall.[3] As I read it, I became gobsmacked at how Catherine and her friends actually seemed to *know* God, not just know about Him. These people talked to Him like He was really there and He apparently spoke back to them! Is that weird or what?

Towards the end of the book, she had a 'prayer of commitment'. I had never heard of this before. To me, commitment meant you believed God existed and tried your best to be good, going 'to church' as much as you could and all that. And I knew church was boring. The way she saw it was that you turned away from the way you had

---

[3] Catherine Marshall, *Beyond Ourselves* (London: Hodder & Stoughton, 1962).

been living, gave yourself totally to God and said you would now follow Him for the rest of your life – that's a commitment a bit like making marriage vows.

I wasn't ready for this kind of thing but something nagged at me deep inside. I was having a good time; really enjoying life and didn't want to have to 'be good', so I decided I would wait till I was old and life was boring anyway. Seems reasonable? I thought so.

Then I had what I can only describe as a 'Mafia moment'. If you've ever seen the film *The Godfather*, which was about the Mafia, you'll know what I mean. The Mafia thugs would tell someone that they would make them an offer they couldn't refuse. That meant, 'You've got a choice – do what I say or die. Which do you prefer?'

God suddenly spoke to me and said, 'Whose terms are you coming on? Yours or Mine?' Now you're going to think *I'm* weird! Was I hearing voices? Well, no, I wasn't. It wasn't like hearing someone talking out loud but a sort of clear sense inside that He was giving me an offer where I had to decide one way or the other. And I was totally aware that my way would not work. I had to decide to follow Him or decide against. Well, really, there was no choice. If I waited till I was old, I would never decide. So, I accepted His offer and just said, 'OK, Lord, I give up!'

Now for some of you, you may think that using ordinary language like that with God is very irreverent. Shouldn't it have been, 'Yea, verily, O Lord, I give myself to Thee' or something equally churchy-sounding? Well, you know what? He's quite OK with us talking to Him in an ordinary way without any of those ancient words such as 'thee'. Jesus spoke in the ordinary language of the people of His time.

I didn't make that decision based on working out if God was there. I was challenged and responded. It was only afterwards that I had to face the evidence questions. My life got turned around and my views on God became very different from when I was a child.

It was quite right that I had ditched my childhood ideas of God – some sort of superhuman up there in 'heaven' – wherever that was. Atheists come to that place if they believed as children. That's where they stop and they think they have then grown up and have a mature attitude to life. Of course, it is more mature than the childish view they had before. So, they think anyone who believes as an adult is still in that childish place. And they are probably right in some cases. Some Christians keep a childish belief all their lives.

However, when I committed my life properly to Christ, I grew up more and realised there was reality beyond what I could see with my eyes. God was beyond all that I had imagined or thought possible. I reckon that is the same for most Christians who have really thought about their belief. That is what atheists cannot understand because they have not grown up in that way and cannot think beyond the science. They only have one angle on life.

For me, as they say, the rest is history. I have been a Christian ever since, although my ideas and understanding have changed massively over the years. I am part of the overall leadership in a church in Glastonbury, Somerset, and have been to Bible college for two years. I have carried on with teaching science as well as maths and ICT (I spent seventeen years out of the classroom in the IT industry). I have also discovered that living as a Christian is far from boring. I hope you will see that as you read the book.

What you are about to read is very much a result of all the things I have had to work through in thinking about God, what He is like and isn't like. It has taken me ages and, if you go on the journey, it will take you ages as well. But I hope what I have got to share with you will help you some of the way.

Introduction

When I was at school, most people believed there was a God, though lots didn't. Nowadays quite a few children in the UK have hardly even heard of Jesus. Also, it seems most people don't think there is a God at all. They think it's just a belief old people have. A large number of people would reckon they were Christians but that is only because they have been christened and confirmed. That is not what makes you a Christian.

I have been for four years to a large get-together of Christians called New Wine[4] in Somerset and I can tell you there are thousands of young people who go there and they have loads of fun. As well as that there are other get-togethers especially for young people called Soul Survivor[5] and Momentum[6] (nothing to do with the Labour Party pressure group), and there are thousands upon thousands who go there. They have a great time.

As I go around schools, I find that even though lots of children don't believe in God, they still want to know why

---

[4] https://www.new-wine.org/ (accessed 11th November 2017).

[5] https://soulsurvivor.com/ (accessed 8th October 2017).

[6] http://momentum.org.uk/ (accessed 8th October 2017).

someone would believe and if there is any proof or evidence for God. Most are open-minded and interested and want to explore it. Those who don't believe reckon science has disproved God and those who do sometimes have beliefs that contradict what they are learning in school, which can cause them quite a lot of hassle in their minds.

So, what is the truth? How do we think clearly about this? I am going to look at this in this book and I'm pleased to have you with me on the journey. It may not always be easy but I hope it will be worth it. I am not writing this to say you have to believe what I say. As you know, I can't make you believe anything anyway and nor can anyone else. You need to make up your own mind.

All I am going to attempt is to give you things to think about that may not have occurred to you before; things to equip you to think critically and examine different arguments. I will have a question for you to think about in each chapter. There is no right or wrong answer to those questions. They are there just to get you thinking, but they could affect the way you think of things in the future. Of course, I hope you will end up believing, but the important thing is that you make an informed decision.

I don't believe there is any conflict between my belief and trust in God and what I know of science, though you may well have heard that the choice is religion or science – you can't have both. I hope to show you in this book that there is no real conflict – you can have both.

1. What Is Atheism?

Let's get technical – always a good thing to look at the dictionary! According to the Oxford Dictionary, atheism is 'Disbelief or lack of belief in the existence of God or gods'.[7]

Atheism has been around for thousands of years. It's not a system or society; just people who can't believe there is a God. Even during Bible times when each nation had its own special god or gods, there were people saying there was no God, so it's nothing new. But I would say that today there are probably more atheists than ever before – especially in the West.

Then there's agnosticism. An agnostic (again according to the Oxford Dictionary) is 'A person who believes that nothing is known or can be known of the existence or nature of God'.[8] Usually we take it to mean someone who says they don't know if there is a God or not. Saying that nothing can be known of the existence or nature of God is a bit silly when you think about it – if I know an earthworm

---

[7] https://en.oxforddictionaries.com/definition/atheism (accessed 10th October 2017).

[8] https://en.oxforddictionaries.com/definition/agnostic (accessed 10th October 2017).

isn't God, I must know a tiny bit about God, even if it's only that He isn't an earthworm!

I'm not going to bother any more about agnosticism except to say that most atheists will admit that they are a little bit agnostic – they can't be absolutely 100 per cent sure there isn't a God because there might just be something they haven't thought about, or a God may be sneaking around in a hidden corner of the universe. That's humility for you!

The reasoning behind atheism

Lots of atheists believe they are more intelligent than religious believers because their lack of belief is based on reasoning, and religions are based on blind trust or instinct. According to *The Independent* newspaper, studies show that 'religious people are less intelligent on average than atheists because faith is an instinct and clever people are better at rising above their instincts'.[9]

That, of course, assumes that religion evolved as an instinct (as far as we know, not one of our closest animal relatives shows the slightest sign of faith at all), that following instincts means lack of intelligence and that believers have not thought about their belief. And, according to Natasha Crain, a statistical geek, the

---

[9] http://www.independent.co.uk/news/science/atheists-more-intelligent-than-religious-people-faith-instinct-cleverness-a7742766.html (accessed 10th October 2017).

conclusions of these studies are highly misleading. Check out this article online in the link.[10]

But what is atheistic reasoning?

They would say:

1. In primitive times, people were trying to find an explanation for how the world and the heavens came about or were created, so they made up stories about gods to explain the origins.

2. As science developed, we began to understand how processes happen and what their causes and results are.

3. We now have scientific explanations for many things and good theories based on observable evidence, so we understand the processes behind creation.

4. We are exploring what we don't know, but are confident it is possible to find explanations for everything.

5. Having scientific explanations means we can do away with any need to make up a God.

They would say children are taught about God creating the world but as you grow up, you realise these are just little childish stories and you need to ditch them. In fact, it

_____

[10] http://crossexamined.org/are-christians-less-intelligent-than-atheists-heres-what-all-those-studies-really-say/ (accessed 10th October 2017).

would be better if children were never told them because they are not true and all you are doing is feeding them with nonsense which confuses them.

The New Atheists

 Most atheists are happy to let people believe in God if they want to. They don't think it does any harm, even though they don't agree with them. 'New Atheists' are something else.

They think superstition, religion and anything like them should be actively countered.[11] They should be exposed for what they are. They think teaching religion to children is indoctrination or even child abuse and should be stopped. They would not like you learning religious education at school. New Atheism is a more extreme form of secular humanism, both of which are organised movements – there are secular humanist societies.

Do you remember Santa? Did he visit you? Maybe he still does. The New Atheists would not approve at all! All it does is confuse you. Are you confused over Santa? If you used to believe in him and now don't, does it make it difficult for you to know what is the truth and what isn't? Do you think your parents lied to you? The New Atheists are concerned that you will not be able to think scientifically if your parents filled your stocking on Christmas Eve and told you Santa was real. And, as for the tooth fairy, well, we had better not go there!

---

[11] Image from https://openclipart.org/detail/286141/religion-is-rubbish (accessed 6th November 2017).

As I go through the book, when I mention atheists, I will really be referring to New Atheists (I just don't want to put the 'New' in every time!) because they are the ones who argue over religion so much.

Richard Dawkins, whom I mentioned earlier, is regarded as the unofficial leader of the New Atheists. He is religiously atheistic and I came across one fan of his who almost worships him. Dawkins wants to convert people. He has little time for other atheists who can't be bothered if people believe in a God. He thinks most people who believe the Bible are stupid and does not seem to be able to understand how some top scientists such as Alister McGrath can have given up their atheism and become Christians. He thinks all religions are anti-scientific, even if they say they accept science. He reckons anyone who is a real scientist and also a Christian should know better.

Professor Dawkins has written some very good books based on scientific research. When he talks about science, he talks sense. His book *The God Delusion* tries to disprove God. He doesn't really know much about God (you wouldn't expect him to do so), but he tries to make out he knows clearly what Christians and people of other religions believe. He doesn't really know and I will show you one reason why.

Speaking about God, he says:

> Either he exists or he doesn't. It is a scientific question; one day we may know the answer, and meanwhile we can say something pretty strong about the probability and the presence or absence

of a creative super-intelligence is unequivocally[12] a scientific question, even if it is not in practice – or not yet – a decided one. So also is the truth or falsehood of every one of the miracle stories that religions rely upon to impress multitudes of the faithful.[13]

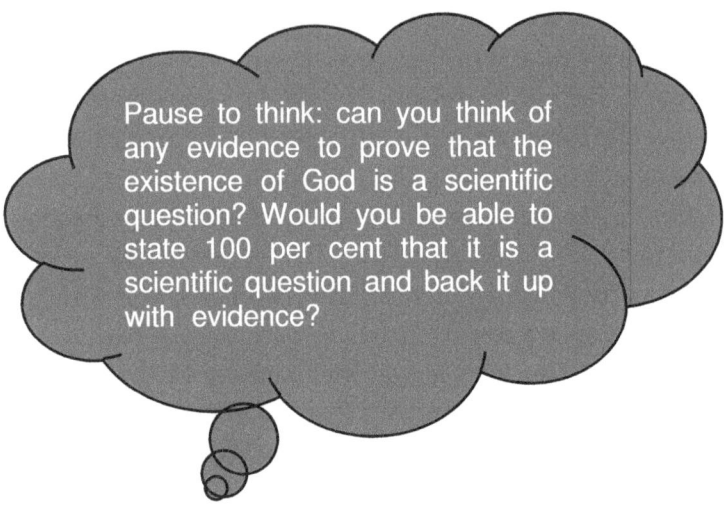

Pause to think: can you think of any evidence to prove that the existence of God is a scientific question? Would you be able to state 100 per cent that it is a scientific question and back it up with evidence?

So, he reckons we can find out through science if God exists or not. He doesn't show why it's a scientific question – he just says it is because he thinks everything is covered by science.

This book is not just about Richard Dawkins, but I will pick on what he says sometimes because he speaks for the

---

[12] Meaning there is no argument about it.

[13] Richard Dawkins, *The God Delusion* (Random House ebooks 2009), p82.

'religious' New Atheists. Let me pick on him now for a moment!

In his book, he assumes that if there is any sort of God, he must be found somewhere in the universe. He goes on to show that this is all but impossible. I totally agree with him, but that is not the God Christians believe in. Christians don't believe God exists as a thing anywhere in the universe, so can't be found by science. To say the existence or non-existence of God is unequivocally a scientific question is, therefore, no more than an opinion on his part, though he would say it is a fact. He has just assumed, without any evidence, that his opinion is correct.

Dawkins uses what is called a straw-man argument. He claims his opponents believe something they don't believe and then disproves their supposed argument. A straw-man argument proves absolutely nothing. As I said in *Even Dawkins Has a God*:

> It sounds convincing but it's a bit like trying to make someone homeless by smashing up a house they don't live in! Easy to do and it may make your fans cheer, but it is quite pointless![14]

---

[14] Neil Laing, *Even Dawkins Has a God* (Bloomington, IN: WestBow Press, 2014), pp42-43.

2. What Is Creationism?

On the whole, through history in the West, most people would have thought of the world as being quite young – you know, a few thousand years or so. Lots also believed that God created animals and plants largely as we see them today. Wasn't that what the Bible said?

Some would have taken the Bible pretty well literally but a lot wouldn't – like Augustine, who is thought of as the 'father' of Christianity in the West. He didn't take it literally, but still believed the world was only a few thousand years old. Most scientists accepted a 'young earth'. But some geologists started finding evidence to suggest the earth was much older.

Then along came Charles Darwin[15] in the nineteenth century. He was training to be a vicar at Cambridge but was also interested in science, and biology especially. He went on a ship called *Beagle* around the

---

15 Image from https://openclipart.org/detail/269679/charles-darwin (accessed 8th November 2017).

world from 1831 to 1836 as a naturalist (what biologists were called in those days). On the journey, he noticed several strange things, especially on the Galapagos Islands in the Pacific, about the animals there – for example, the finches and mockingbirds. (Scientists have actually now discovered a new species of finch on the Galapagos Islands that has arisen since 1981. Check this BBC link to read the report.[16])

He also noticed lines of shells embedded in rock about fifteen metres above the sea on Santiago, suggesting the land had gradually risen over a very long time. If it had risen quickly, the shells would have been messed up.

After this journey, he wrote that famous book, *On the Origin of Species*, where he showed that organisms had come about by a process he called natural selection. This had resulted in an evolutionary process which gave rise to all life – things that we see today and everything that has become extinct, originating from very simple organisms.

Charles Darwin partially abandoned his faith but still thought of himself as a Christian. He seemed to keep his belief in the existence of God but came to distrust the Bible – probably because he was previously convinced it should be taken literally, as were most scientists of his day. He became convinced it was, therefore, unreliable and would say he was more agnostic.

To start with, the Church was not too bothered about this new theory and many scientists discarded it. But very soon, a prominent atheist, Thomas Huxley, used it to show that God was now not necessary to explain creation.

---

[16] http://www.bbc.co.uk/news/science-environment-42103058 (accessed 3rd December 2017).

The Church reacted by trying to discredit the theory. Lots of Christians started to affirm that God had created all things and that it had happened only a few thousand years before, rather than the hundreds of millions of years required by evolution.

But evolution has now become very much mainstream science and very few scientists reject it. Those who reject it are known as creationists. A large proportion of Christians and lots of Muslims are creationists.

Christian creationism does vary quite a lot but there are three main streams. They all say God created everything much as we see them today. The three main streams are:

1. Those who believe the universe is 6,000 (or to a maximum of 10,000) years old; that each day mentioned in Genesis 1 is a literal twenty-four-hour day.

2. Those who say the days may be non-literal and could represent long periods of time or ages.

3. Those who say the words 'the earth *was* without form and void'[17] could also mean 'the world *became* without form and void' so that there could have been an initial creation a long time ago, then everything was destroyed and a new creation started 6,000 years ago.

In this book, I will ignore the last two and concentrate on the first when discussing creationism because that is the main belief of creationists, and what I say about that will largely apply to the other two anyway.

---

[17] Genesis 1:2 (ESV, my italics).

Pause to think: do you think it is possible to believe the Bible and believe in evolution and the Big Bang? If so, how? If not, why not?

Now that you know what these positions are, we can get going on the arguments. But, as you may have gathered, I don't agree with either atheism or creationism. I just like to be awkward!

Actually, being awkward, I think 'creationist' is the wrong word. How about people who believe God creates everything, but through an evolutionary process? Aren't they 'creationists'? But I suppose we've got to stick with the words people generally use. If you see that word, at least you know what it means to most people. And I will use it in that sense.

3. Has Science Thrown the Bible on the Rubbish Heap?

Literally sitting in front of me as I write this is a teacher doing a day of supply. I mentioned to her that I was writing this book and she said, 'I always thought it was either science or religion; that you can't have both. This is fascinating – I have never seen it like that before.' She is not a science teacher, by the way. (And I have told her what I have written about her!)

I'm sure you've heard people say that. You may even think it. Lots of people do. Almost all atheists believe it. A few are more open-minded and say it is possible that science may find God.

Of course, this is based on what I said earlier – the belief that we now have science to explain everything, so we don't need God or the Bible.

Professor Dawkins insists it is a scientific question as to whether there is a God or not.[18] As he sees it, everything has to be covered by science. Nothing is true if it cannot be shown to be true scientifically.

---

[18] Dawkins, *The God Delusion*, p82.

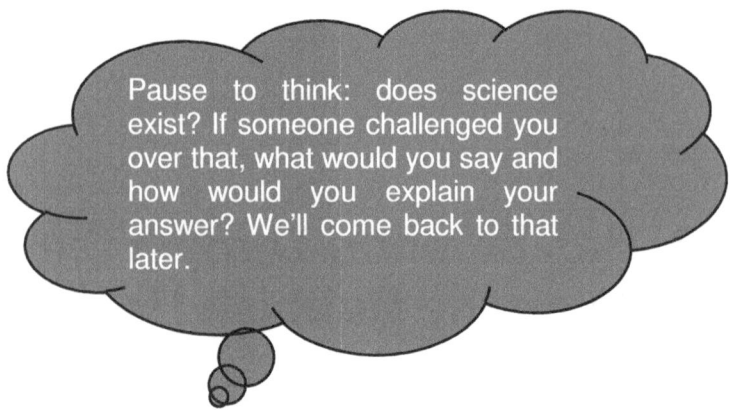

Pause to think: does science exist? If someone challenged you over that, what would you say and how would you explain your answer? We'll come back to that later.

When you think about it, there is a sort of agreement between atheists and creationists.

Atheists believe the Bible is an attempt at a scientific explanation. Creationists say it *is* the scientific explanation.

Atheists accept mainstream science and believe the Bible has childish, out-of-date science; creationists believe the 'science' in the Bible is correct and that real science agrees with it. They believe most scientists have wrong interpretations of science, based on their atheism, and that Christians who accept evolution are compromisers.

Is the Bible a science book?

There was no such thing as science when any of the Bible was written. It was in the nineteenth century when William Whewell used the word 'science' to distinguish people who sought knowledge on nature from those who sought other kinds of knowledge. Whewell was a Christian, a very prominent scientist and had an influence on Charles Darwin.

So, if the Bible was written before there was any science, is it anti-science or is it sort of completely unscientific? Well, it is neither. We need to see what sort of book the Bible really is.

I think it must be obvious to anyone reading it that the Bible cannot be called a science book. It's not unscientific, but it is non-scientific. Its main message is not to explain mechanisms to us, but to be God's communication with us. And, most importantly, it's about God giving us some idea of what He is like.

But look! Science can only throw out more ancient science; it can show it is false; it can reveal new things. As the Bible is non-scientific, it can't be thrown out by any science, though some parts can be tested scientifically – for instance, by archaeology.

If God is as the Bible shows us, then there is no way any book can tell us all there is to know about Him. But the Bible is written is such a way that for those who are open-minded, God can expand their horizons to see beyond those words and peer into the 'mystery' of who He is. I know some atheists will think 'mystery' just means stuff that is beyond evidence and is 'mysterious', but that is not what it means at all. 'Mystery' means things that we cannot simply work out with plain logic – we need insight which, in understanding the Bible, comes from God.

The Bible is written as history, as theology, as poetry, as allegory, as metaphor and in all sorts of different styles of writing. It is not meant to enlighten the casual reader, and it's not meant to enlighten those who treat it only as ancient literature. But for those who truly want to see, it can reveal some amazing wisdom about life and living.

Many creationists insist it all has to be taken literally, but I have found that if you do that, you will be robbed of countless gems. Yes, of course some of it is literal; some is obviously not, and some of it we may not know whether it should be literal or not. Am I bothered? I don't think we have to work out every passage to decide on how it should be treated – otherwise it becomes a textbook, and that is definitely not what it is.

The Bible is looking at people, the world and life, as does science, but is doing so from a completely different angle.

 Science is constantly trying to get a better and better view on how things work[19] – matter, energy, force and so on. It's trying to explain things from that angle. It can deal with all those things – basically, anything that can be measured in the entire universe. That is one huge amount of knowledge.

How about poetry, though? How about abstract art? Can you measure love? If I love my wife with all my heart, does that mean I have nothing left for my children? Some atheists will tell you that love does not really exist. In a way, they are right. It doesn't exist in a scientific way, but I wouldn't dare tell my wife that my love for her was just an illusion!

Can you imagine a boy in love with a girl and he says to her, 'I've had some tests done by the doctor and it appears

---

[19] Image from https://openclipart.org/detail/280698/using-a-telescope (accessed 8th November 2017).

my dopaminergic subcortical system[20] becomes very active when I am around you. According to what I understand, that means I am attracted to you.' She'd certainly find that romantic, wouldn't she? I don't think so! But it is true scientifically.

The Bible does not look at life in that way at all, but that doesn't mean it's not true. It's just looking from a different angle. Let's illustrate it like this:

Think about a rainbow for a moment. A rainbow is formed when the light is refracted by raindrops (split into its various colours of red, orange, yellow, green, blue, indigo and violet) forming a semicircular bow in the sky. I have described a rainbow for you. But is that all there is to it?

Can't I say a rainbow[21] is beautiful? That's non-scientific (but not unscientific). If I am a Christian, can't I also say it's revealing a glimpse of the glory of God? I can't prove either of the last two interpretations but that doesn't mean they aren't true. I am sure you at least believe the first is true.

Can you see that non-scientific interpretations can still be true? They are just looking from another point of view.

---

[20] I will not explain this but I'm not making it up – look at https://www.bustle.com/articles/85844-what-happens-when-you-fall-in-love-8-surprising-things-that-happen-to-your-body-because (accessed 10th October 2017).

[21] Image from https://openclipart.org/detail/178746/cute-rain-cloud-with-rainbow (accessed 8th November 2017).

Think about poetry. Here's one I loved as a boy by Alfred Lord Tennyson called 'The Eagle':

> He clasps the crag with crooked hands
> Close to the sun in lonely lands
> Ring'd with the azure world he stands.
>
> The wrinkled sea beneath him crawls
> He watches from his mountain walls
> And, like a thunderbolt, he falls.[22]

Is it true? Analyse it scientifically and you'll see it's rubbish. Eagles don't have hands; they're no closer to the sun than you are; the waves on the sea have particles that go around in circles – they don't crawl. Mountains don't have walls and eagles don't fall like thunderbolts. But it still gives you a truthful picture of an eagle. That's something like the Bible – lots of it cannot be analysed scientifically, but it is telling you the truth.

When it comes to the history bits, you need to remember we think of history as being in date order. History in the Bible was written to talk about God's dealings with people; some of it may be in the wrong order; lots of it is left out, and what is there is emphasising the 'God' angle so it doesn't read like your history textbook. They were not writing it as a modern historical account for your school history course.

So, the Bible is not a book to learn like a textbook; it's not an academic book. It's designed to lead the reader to

---

[22] https://www.poetryfoundation.org/poems/45322/the-eagle-56d224c9a41d1 (accessed 12th October 2017).

know God – a very different thing from trying to get you a degree in theology.

Before we leave this chapter, let's think about the question I asked you earlier. I asked if science exists. I don't know what you think, but if it does, where is it? What does it look like? Can we measure it? Could you search the universe and find science? You'd find scientific processes everywhere, but you wouldn't find science anywhere. You see, science doesn't exist as a thing. It's a method; a way of thinking, experimenting and finding out about the universe. It's not a thing, but it is certainly real. Now, what does that tell you about God?

4. Can We Trust the Bible?

It's all very well to say that the Bible is not all meant to be taken literally, that some is literal, some is poetic, etc. But can we trust what it says? Is it really the truth? Surely with all these miracles (parting the Red Sea, people being raised from the dead and so on) it has to be exaggerated.

There have been people throughout history trying to disprove the Bible – often saying that what it claims is impossible, or that people in those days, who didn't have science, explained things as miracles. Then they will say that books with prophetic statements were written after the event but that the writers wrote them *as if* it was before the event.

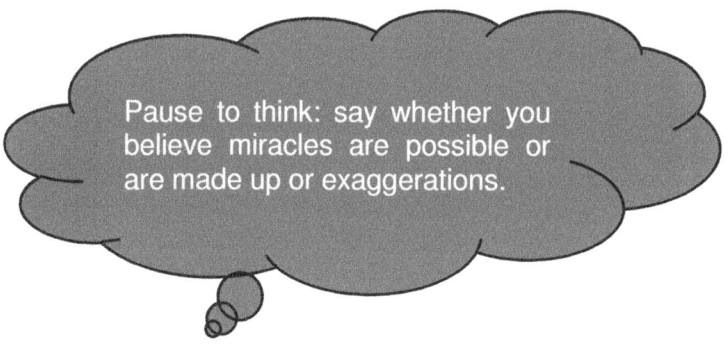

Pause to think: say whether you believe miracles are possible or are made up or exaggerations.

I listened to an archaeologist, Professor Alan Millard, a couple of weeks ago. He has spent more than fifty years in his profession. He was quite honest and said there were a number of things in the Bible that had not (at least yet) been shown to be correct archaeologically, but he said that wherever we have clear evidence, everything confirms what the Bible says. So that suggests we can be pretty confident it is true.

Prophetic claims

The Old Testament is full of prophecies (many of which foretell the future). Some of these are not very obvious; some are put in symbolic language and some are plain. I cannot possibly go into all of these – it would mean a huge book – but I will look at a couple of examples.

The prophet Isaiah lived more than 700 years before Christ, but gave prophecies anticipating He would appear. These prophecies are scattered through the book but this is a well-known one:

> So, the Master is going to give you a sign anyway. Watch for this: A girl who is presently a virgin[23] will get pregnant. She'll bear a son, and name him Immanuel (God-With-Us).[24]

Now, a young girl giving birth is nothing remarkable – hardly a sign of anything. But a virgin cannot give birth. You know your biology and you know that it takes a male

---

[23] 'Virgin' here means a young unmarried girl.
[24] Isaiah 7:14 (MSG).

and female to produce a baby (and they had no in-vitro fertilisation in those days).

Then he says she will call His name Immanuel, which means 'God with us'. The Hebrews used to name their children hoping that the name they gave them would be what they turned out to be. To suggest that a baby would be God with us would have been highly offensive to the Hebrews. But Isaiah says this would be the Lord giving the sign, not some crackpot girl with delusions of grandeur.

In the New Testament, we then find that a young girl (probably around sixteen years old) called Mary was chosen by God to bear a very special baby, Jesus – who, it is claimed, was the Son of God and that, in Him, God lived among us (God with us). Pretty amazing claims, but if true, they are a direct fulfilment of Isaiah's prophecy.

Later, the prophet Zechariah said:

> Then the LORD said to me, 'Throw it to the potter'—the lordly price at which I was priced by them. So I took the thirty pieces of silver and threw them into the house of the LORD, to the potter.[25]

Here God is saying the people valued Him (God) at thirty pieces of silver (about four month's wages for a labourer, and the penalty that should be paid to the owner of a slave if someone's ox gored the slave to death).

In the New Testament, we find Judas being paid thirty pieces of silver to betray Jesus. And, when he realised that what he had done was utterly wrong, he threw the money

---

[25] Zechariah 11:13 (ESV).

into the temple (the house of the Lord) and the priests used the money to buy the potter's field.[26]

Zechariah prophesied more than 500 years before Christ. How could he have known that sort of detail? Imagine living 500 years or 700 years ago and someone accurately predicting what was going to happen today. We hardly even know what is going to happen tomorrow. Even the weather forecast is often wrong!

The Old Testament has loads of such predictions, many of which have already been fulfilled. I don't know many other books like that. Do you?

Miracles

Ah, but some of the miracles are ridiculous, you might say (or maybe you don't!). Some of them do seem pretty far-fetched, I grant you. Things such as axe-heads floating on water, or people coming back to life after dying, or the sun delaying its setting for nearly a whole day, or even going backwards once. We may think modern medicine is incredible, but some of the miracles in both the Old and New Testaments are beyond amazing. Surely the fact that we don't see anything like that happening today means it is all just made up?

Well, I will look at modern miracles in chapter 11 but I can tell you they are happening today and that, to me, is sufficient to tell me that the ones I read about in the Bible are perfectly possible. I am not aware of the sun turning back, but God never does things for show, and I cannot

---

[26] Matthew 26:15; 27:3-8.

imagine there has ever been another time when there was a need for something like that to happen.[27]

If we are talking about axe-heads floating,[28] then I would say that if people can walk on water, making an axe-head float on water is just as easy. Jesus walked on water and the apostle Peter did for a short time before he got scared,[29] but it happens today as well. You can hear about it in this YouTube clip referenced below where some people in Indonesia walked across a swollen river[30] without realising they were in a miracle at the time.

I came across another amazing story of a rescue where a lady is rescued from her car underwater and there is something in it that can't be explained. You can hear about it in this YouTube clip.[31]

Then there's the one about God making a path through the Red Sea for the Israelites to go through. You may have seen pictures in children's Bibles with a wall of water on each side of them.

I am not sure exactly what happened in that particular incident, but it says God sent a wind blowing all night and it drove the waters back. It does say the water was a wall on each side, but they used the word 'wall' to mean protection, so it was possibly that He removed the water to each side by using a strong wind. It may not have been

---

[27] Joshua 10:13.

[28] See the story in 2 Kings 6:1-7.

[29] Matthew 14:22-33.

[30] https://www.youtube.com/watch?v=93TKE8_4QC0 (13th October 2017).

[31] https://www.youtube.com/watch?v=4wQglesZdQo (2nd December 2017).

standing up in walls like in those pictures, but I believe there was a path through the sea. When the Egyptians tried to follow, the waters suddenly returned to cover and drown them.[32]

How about the healing miracles in the Bible?

When it comes to healings, I have no problem in believing that the miracles in the Bible are true. I have seen so many amazing healings with my own eyes that I cannot doubt them. There are literally thousands happening every single day right now across the world.

Jesus is said to have raised three people from the dead (one of them, Lazarus, had been dead for four days).[33] Doctors have brought people back to life, but only after they have been dead for a very short time, and that is with modern medical methods. Jesus just commanded these people to rise up. Surely that is made up. I cannot claim to have seen anyone raised from the dead myself, but I have heard of a number of instances of it happening in our time.

So, in answer to the question 'Can we trust the Bible?', I would say that, while we cannot prove everything in the Bible because it all happened so long ago, the evidence we have strongly suggests that it is trustworthy. The other thing is it is very much calling on us to be truthful and honest – it would be a bit rich if it was entirely dishonest.

---

[32] Exodus 14.
[33] Read the story in John 11.

We will look at evidence for God in chapter 13, but now I want to look at what so many people think – that the Bible and science are against each other.

5. But the Bible and Science Are against Each Other

Archbishop Ussher (1581-1656) calculated that the date of creation was Saturday 22nd October 4004 BC at about 6pm.[34] In the Hebrew way of counting days, 6pm is the start of the next day, so this would actually be the start of Sunday. Creationists reckon that the world and the universe are 6,000 years old – or at the most about 10,000 years.

They do not say science and the Bible are against each other, but that most scientists completely misinterpret science (either deliberately or by mistake) and that the creationist interpretation of science is the only one that is correct. They say evolution has not taken place – well, they would say evolution 'within kinds' is possible but, for example, an amphibian could not turn into a reptile. Some say each species is a separate kind.

Unfortunately, it's a bit difficult to say what a 'kind' is and the Bible isn't much help there either. Creationists are

---

[34] If you want to read a creationist account of this, look at https://answersingenesis.org/bible-timeline/the-world-born-in-4004-bc/ (accessed 11th October 2017).

keen on putting animals we know well into 'kinds', such as a 'dog kind' and a 'cat kind', but I wonder if they include lions, tigers and leopards in 'cat kind' and does the 'dog kind' include wolves, bears and coyotes? Some of them will include a 'mammal kind' as well, but dogs and cats are mammals, so are dogs in the 'dog kind' or the 'mammal kind'? Animals they don't know so well are put in larger groups like 'bird kind', 'reptile kind' and so on. You wonder if they reckon a budgie could evolve into an ostrich, being in the same kind! Is that a scientific way of classifying things? I hardly think so. It sounds good to people who don't know any better but ridiculous to anyone who knows biology.

Basically, a creationist thinks that believing God made each species suddenly[35] and specially means you accept Him as Creator. If you think they may have come about by any other process, that means God didn't do it. That is why they are so anti-evolution. To me, that means you would have to believe that anything with a proven scientific explanation does not involve God so He is only responsible for the things we don't understand. That is called a 'God of the gaps' and, I would say, is very bad theology.

Listen! Don't believe everything someone tells you. Don't believe something just because I tell you, either. I am

[35] https://openclipart.org/detail/16122/adam-eve-happy (accessed 8th November 2017).

sure you have been and are being taught at school to question what you are told. That's very good advice but the trouble is when you are a teenager, you don't have nearly as much knowledge as an adult and so you don't have so much to test things against. A few teenagers think they know everything, but you will learn loads more as you go through your life. You need to gain knowledge and different ways of looking at life so that you can see 'the bigger picture' and test one thing against another.

What I want to do in this chapter is show you some other ways of looking at this problem and then, hopefully, you can make a better judgement. Then in the next two chapters, I will go on to show you how the Bible can be believed alongside 'normal' science.

The Bible

I've talked about rainbows and eagles earlier. There are different ways of regarding rainbows, and poems can tell us the truth without being scientifically true.

The Bible account in the first chapters of Genesis (and in many other places) is not necessarily literally true. A day may not mean twenty-four hours. The order may not be exact.

There is strong evidence that it was written in an ancient Hebrew style of poetry. Look at the repeating sentences ('there was evening and there was morning').[36] It wasn't written as an explanation of creation, but to give us a truthful picture of the fact that God was responsible for it. I can say 'it is the word of God' even though it may not be

---

[36] Genesis 1:5, 8, 13, 19, 23, 31 (ESV).

literally and scientifically true. I believe it was never meant as an explanation but as a statement.

Pause to think: would Adam and Eve have been created as adults or as new-born babies? Either way, what would this imply?

Adam and Eve

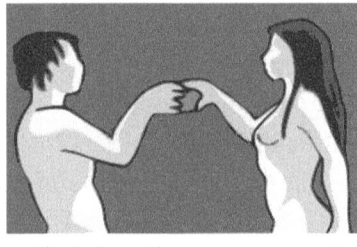

Was there a literal Adam and Eve or is it just made up? I can't say but some people think they were Neolithic farmers.[37] I very much doubt if they were called by those names, however. The fifth chapter of Genesis mentions that God made people male and female and called *their* name 'Adam'.[38]

---

[37] Dr Denis Alexander wrote *Creation or Evolution: Do We Have to Choose?* (Oxford: Monarch, 2008):
https://en.wikipedia.org/wiki/Denis_Alexander (accessed 11th October 2017).
[38] Genesis 5:1-2.

Was it a single couple or several people? I just don't know, but it doesn't bother me. Maybe it shouldn't bother you. But then there's that 'apple'.[39] Firstly, it wasn't an apple. It was the fruit of the tree of the knowledge of good and evil. I really cannot imagine that is a literal tree. And God said if they ate it, they would surely die that day.[40] They ate it and lived for hundreds more years!

What are we to make of all this? I cannot be sure I am right at all and I very much doubt if I am, but the way I see it is that God took creatures which were highly intelligent animals and breathed into them the breath of life so that they became living souls.[41] I don't see that as physical life because He didn't do it with any other animals and they were all alive. It was a different kind of life that made this animal able to know God and meant it was now completely different from all other animals. The difference was not physical – we are incredibly close to chimpanzees biologically; it was spiritual – an ability to know God.

We read that the devil[42] tempted Adam and Eve. Firstly, he questioned God's command, asking if there was anything God had forbidden them to eat (nothing like concentrating on the negative). Eve replied that God had said they could eat from any tree except the tree in the middle of the garden, or they would die. The devil then flatly contradicted God and said they would not die. God

---

[39] Image from https://openclipart.org/detail/286950/adam-and-eve (accessed 8th November 2017).

[40] Genesis 2:16-17.

[41] Genesis 2:7.

[42] I won't get into whether or not the devil is real (that's not what this is about), but he is seen as the very spirit of evil.

knew, he said, that they would then become familiar with good and evil, not just good – they would become educated! God was being a spoilsport.[43]

When they became aware of good and evil because they saw it as being good education,[44] they lost this life God had breathed into them and died, though they were still very much physically alive. They lost the relationship with Him and life became a drag. But they didn't die completely. God left ways for them to be able to get right with Him again and many people sought Him and found Him.

Just quickly – do I think the devil was a snake? I reckon that was symbolic. Many snakes are poisonous and it seems an appropriate picture to use of evil. I feel sorry that snakes have had a very bad press ever since. I used to keep some in my shirt at school and they were always fine. They get tame very quickly.

To get back to my earlier question: were Adam and Eve born as babies or adults?

If Adam and Eve were born as babies, who would have taken care of them? This is certainly not implied in the text in the Bible.

If they were born as adults, they would appear to be a few years old but would actually have only just been created, so they would deceptively appear to be older than they were.

Which scenario do you think fits better? Is what I suggested before reasonable or not? If we do not take it all as a literal scientific account, could it make sense? Could it still be telling us the truth?

---

[43] Genesis 3:4-5.

[44] Genesis 3:6.

The Big Bang

Well, surely the Big Bang completely disproves the Bible?
We will have a look at that in the next chapter.

6. Big Bang or Sudden Creation?

Disagreement among Christians

Before we move on, let me make it clear that Christians do not all speak with one voice on the whole question of science and faith. There are lots of views. As far as I am concerned, as long as anyone has genuine biblical and scientific evidence to support what they believe, I respect their view, whether or not I agree with them. I will really be amazed if I find I am completely right. You need to believe because you genuinely believe, not because someone else tells you.

Where did the universe come from?

Creationists believe God created first the earth in a day; then the sun, moon and stars in a day, and all the plants and animals on earth each in a moment on a couple of other days. This belief is especially true in America. A number of Christians think that if you disagree with it, you cannot be a true Christian. To them, evolution is seen as the doctrine of devils.

A little bit of history

Scientists used to think that matter was 'eternal' – because if there was a time when there was no matter, there would have been a vacuum, and a vacuum is impossible. There is a law in chemistry stating that matter can neither be created nor destroyed. That is true in normal circumstances and is used to work out the reactants and products in chemical reactions.

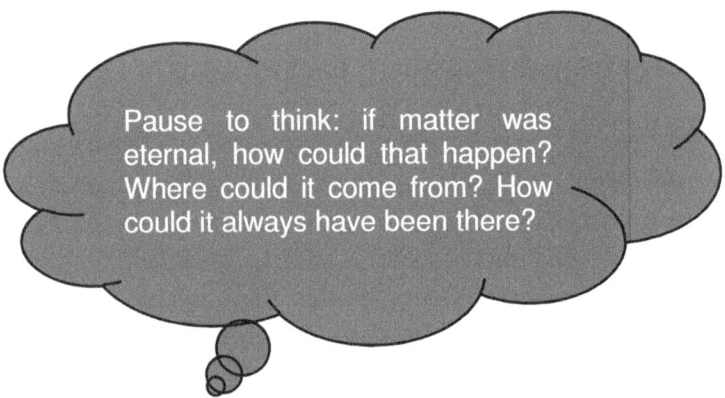

Pause to think: if matter was eternal, how could that happen? Where could it come from? How could it always have been there?

However, we now know that matter can be created through quantum mechanical processes – that energy and matter can be interchangeable (that's an example of laws we thought were definite now having to be qualified in some way).

Scientists who believed matter was eternal would have said the statement 'In the beginning, God created the heavens and the earth'[45] was nonsense because there was no beginning.

---

[45] Genesis 1:1 (ESV).

Then a Monsignor Georges Lemaître, a Belgian Roman Catholic priest, using observations other people had made on galaxies getting further and further from the earth, reckoned there must have been a beginning from a tiny point.

To begin with, most scientists rejected his idea. Sir Fred Hoyle, a famous English astronomer, thought it was nonsense and called it 'the Big Bang' theory to mock it.[46] Atheists didn't like it because it meant there would have to be a beginning. However, they quickly realised it filled a gap (the 'who created the universe in the first place?' gap). So, they accepted this theory and used it to try to discredit God.

According to the Big Bang Theory, about 13.8 billion years ago, there was no universe as we know it – just a tiny point with zero volume (i.e. nothing, not even space or time) and then this suddenly started expanding at speeds faster than light (there was no light at first), and this expansion is still happening. Scientists have now collected loads of data to show that this makes sense.[47] Although we can't be 100 per cent certain, there is a lot of evidence for the theory.

Instead of attacking the wrong assumptions of the atheists, Christians reacted by attacking the Big Bang Theory. But did you know the Bible uses language that, in a poetic way, could support the Big Bang Theory? In lots of

---

[46] https://www.theguardian.com/news/2001/aug/23/guardianobituaries.spaceexploration (accessed 31st October 2017).
[47] http://www.nationalgeographic.com/science/space/universe/origins-of-the-universe/ (accessed 12th October 2017).

places, it says God created and 'stretched out' the heavens.[48]

Big Bang – Big Battle

That's the problem. Many atheists completely misunderstand what God is all about, as I have tried to show in previous chapters; creationists attack what they see as false science instead of the wrong ideas on the part of atheists. The only problem between believing God created the universe and the Big Bang is the time. If you believe the universe is 6,000 years old, the Big Bang is out of the question. But if you accept Genesis chapter 1 as a statement and poetry, that the days are not literal, the problem melts away. Both the Big Bang Theory and the Bible say there was a beginning. One looks at it scientifically; the other looks at it poetically and theologically.

Big Balance; minute precision

Brian Cox (a very nice atheist) acknowledges that the chance of the universe being exactly right for life is extremely small. He doesn't say how small. To explain how it could be exactly right, he suggests there could be an almost infinite number of universes; that we are completely unaware of the others and we just happen to live in one that supports life. But there is no evidence of

---

[48] Job 9:8; Isaiah 42:5; 44:24; 45:12; 51:13; Jeremiah 10:12; 51:15; Zechariah 12:1 (ESV).

any other universe, so that is a faith position on his part. How small is the chance?

The balance between the force of the Big Bang making the universe expand and the contracting force (gravity) preventing it from going too fast has to be so exact that the chance of it being exactly right is about the same as the chance of firing a beam of light and hitting a particular 1cm square at the edge of the universe without looking. Theoretically that could have happened by pure chance, but I would say it's just as reasonable if not more reasonable to suggest it was intended to be like that. The balance right at the start of the Big Bang had to be even more exact. It would be 1 in 10 to the power of so much that there would be nowhere near enough atoms in the entire universe to write all the zeroes, even if there was one zero on each atom.[49] That is some accuracy! Dr Paul Davies, professor of theoretical physics at the University of Adelaide, put it this way:

> The really amazing thing is not that life on Earth is balanced on a knife-edge, but that the entire universe is balanced on a knife-edge, and would be total chaos if any of the natural 'constants' were off even slightly. You see, even if you

---

[49] If you want to know what that number is, it's 1:10 to the power of 10 to the power of 123. That means a 1 with 1,000 trillion trillion trillion trillion trillion trillion trillion trillion trillion trillion zeroes. They reckon there are between 10^{78} and 10^{82} atoms in the universe. That's 10 billion trillion trillion trillion trillion trillion trillion atoms. So, there would be 100 000 trillion trillion trillion trillion times as many zeroes as there are atoms in the whole universe.

dismiss man as a chance happening, the fact remains that the universe seems unreasonably suited to the existence of life – almost contrived – you might say a 'put-up job'.[50]

Which is more reasonable? That there are an infinite number of universes with no evidence for them, or what Professor Davies suggests? And if he is right, who put the job up?

Ah, but how about evolution?

---

[50] http://www.simpletoremember.com/articles/a/science-quotes/ (accessed 10th October 2017).

7. Doesn't Evolution Disprove Creation?

As I write this bit, I am spending a week at an event in the south-west of England called New Wine, on the Christians in Science stand. We are talking to people about science and faith. Just the other day, a girl said that, of course, Christians couldn't really get into science because it disagreed with Christianity. Another wanted to do ophthalmology (study of eyes) but was worried because she'd have to learn about the evolution of the eye!

That is sad, sad, sad!

Many years ago, I heard of a man in Pretoria, South Africa, who asked to see the human fossils in the museum and then started smashing them up. He was stopped, fortunately, before he had done massive damage, but he said they had been created by the devil to deceive people! I never thought the devil could create anything.

For creationists, evolution is where anger rises. I had another man at the New Wine event tell me that the theory of evolution was 'from the pit of hell'. He wasn't a scientist. Just after that another man came along and asked if we accepted evidence-based science when dealing with the question. We told him we did and he was relieved, saying he could not accept creationism! Two Christians; two very different views.

The theory of evolution is an attempt to explain how living things change[51] and new species come about over time, while creation is a statement telling us who is behind everything that happens. They do not have to be opposed to each other.

If creationism is true – that God created all things suddenly in a mature state in six literal twenty-four-hour days 6,000 years ago, then there is war! If that is what faith requires, then it is science vs faith.

Creation is a scientific question, while the existence or non-existence of God is not. We have to look at things that exist like living things from a scientific point of view if we

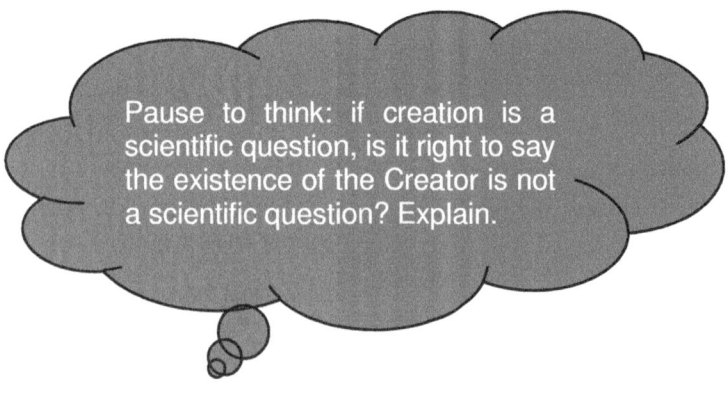

Pause to think: if creation is a scientific question, is it right to say the existence of the Creator is not a scientific question? Explain.

[51] Image from https://openclipart.org/detail/215201/evolution (accessed 8th November 2017).

are to understand how they came about. Scientists must be free from having to follow any Bible interpretation in exploring nature.

In my battle to understand this seeming conflict between creation and evolution, I noticed some very interesting similarities between the Bible account and science. I've already mentioned how God is said to have created and stretched out the heavens. Now let's look at the creation of the solar system, the earth and of life on it.

The evolution of the earth

According to scientific theory, around 9 billion years (give or take a few hundred million) after the start of the Big Bang, large blobs of gas formed as parts of a solar system. One of these (earth) was humungously hot but cooled gradually, eventually becoming solid probably around 3½ billion years ago.

The Bible account

The second verse of the Bible says, 'The earth was without form and void, and darkness was over the face of the deep. And the spirit of God was hovering over the face of the waters.'[52]

If the earth came from gases orbiting the sun as we think it did – then cooling to form liquid and then solid, it would have been without form to start with, as the Bible suggests. The idea of the Spirit of God hovering is difficult to fit into a scientific account, but it isn't supposed to be scientific; it's

---

[52] Genesis 1:2 (ESV).

a theological statement. It's telling us who is responsible for what happened, not how it happened.

Verses 3 to 5 say:

> And God said, 'Let there be light', and there was light. And God saw that the light was good. And God separated the light from the darkness. God called the light Day, and the darkness he called Night. And there was evening and there was morning, the first day.[53]

If the young hot earth was surrounded by masses of water vapour (thick clouds), it would have been impossible to see the sun, but it would have been possible to see light and darkness. The creation of sun and moon is only mentioned on day four. We can assume this account would be from the point of view of seeing it from earth.

Verses 6 to 8 say:

> And God said, 'Let there be an expanse in the midst of the waters, and let it separate the waters from the waters.' And God made the expanse and separated the waters that were under the expanse from the waters that were above the expanse. And it was so. And God called the expanse Heaven. And there was evening and there was morning, the second day.[54]

When the earth was very hot, any rain falling would have evaporated but as it cooled, water would have started

---

[53] ESV.
[54] ESV.

to lie on the surface so the water vapour in the sky would be separated from the water on the surface.

Then verses 9 and 10 say:

> And God said, 'Let the waters under the heavens be gathered together into one place, and let the dry land appear.' And it was so. God called the dry land Earth, and the waters that were gathered together he called Seas. And God saw that it was good.[55]

Then the earth would have started to shrink and buckle as it cooled so dry land and seas (oceans) would appear. It was becoming suitable for life to start. Of course, all this would have taken a couple of billion years, not days, but otherwise this fits well with what we could imagine happening on an evolving earth.

Evolution of life

According to what we think scientifically, proteins formed in a sort of 'soup' of chemicals and these proteins came together to form more complex structures. At some stage, they developed the ability to reproduce or replicate themselves and so became the basis of life.

Then, about 541 million years ago, these very simple precursors of living things suddenly (over about 53 million years) exploded into loads and loads of different life forms – in what we call the Cambrian period. The first examples

---

[55] ESV.

of each of most of the major groups of animals and plants we know today were found in the Cambrian period.

Then over the ensuing hundreds of millions of years, the earth changed dramatically and we ended up with the kind of life we see today through a process of evolution.

Biblical account

The formation of seas and the emergence of plants are recorded on day three – before the sun, moon and stars were created on day four.

 I would imagine there would have been enough of a break in the clouds for the heavenly bodies to be seen before life started, so the order does not fit exactly, but it does mention plants before animals and, of course, with plants being the producers in food webs, they would have to evolve before animals.

Then in verses 20 to 22 on day five, the sea creatures and 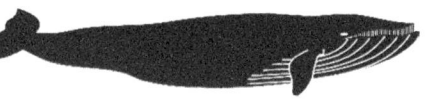 birds are created. All sea creatures are lumped together, whereas we know mammals (whales,[56] etc.) would have evolved late and so would the birds. However, we are also pretty sure that life started in the seas.

Finally, on day six, we have the creation of land animals and humanity (no mention of Adam and Eve in chapter 1). Again, we are pretty sure land animals evolved from those in the sea.

You may notice, if you read the account in Genesis, that God says, 'Let the earth sprout...' and then we read 'the earth brought forth'[57] and so on. This sounds like the non-living world was involved in producing life – which is true.

So, far from the Bible and science being opposed to each other, they actually agree amazingly, especially if you don't get all hung up on the time and the exact order but see the biblical account as a poem which is not trying to give us an explanation, but looking at creation from a different angle.

Science and faith, I believe, help each other. There are similarities between them, but there is an advantage in understanding life from different angles. How boring it would be to think of rainbows in terms of refraction of light only; how much we would lack understanding if we always thought they were there just to give us a beautiful sight.

---

[56] Image from https://openclipart.org/detail/173515/whale-by-rones (accessed 8th November 2017).
[57] Genesis 1:11-12 (ESV).

About our pause to think question: I would say that as science is only studying the creation, it cannot decide on whether or not the Creator exists, but if He does, it may be able to tell us a lot about Him – in a similar way that studying a piece of art can tell us something about the artist.

Some people describe it this way: God inspired two books – (1) the Bible and (2) nature. Both of these books tell us about the Creator.

8. Does Science Tell Us 'How' and Faith Tell Us 'Why'?

We are very used to seeing that everything has a purpose. But often we go too far. You may occasionally hear someone say, for example, 'Fishes developed lungs so that they could live on land.' That is scientific rubbish! The truth is that some fishes (things like mudskippers) developed lungs and so they were able to live partly out of the water. But no fish thought, 'I think I'll develop lungs so I can live on land.'

Let's try this. Concentrate hard and try to develop wings (just tiny ones to start with!).[58] Are you concentrating hard enough? The evidence will be the start of wings. Nothing? Obviously, you're not trying hard enough. Try again. Close your eyes and push where you think the wings should emerge. Still nothing? Oh well, you know I'm just making a point.

---

[58] Image from https://pixabay.com/en/angel-baby-cherub-leaning-1299460/ (accessed 25th November 2017).

As far as science is concerned, there is no purpose in existence. We are just here. As far as biology is concerned, the ultimate function of an organism (plant/animal) is to reproduce itself so that its genes continue. I have three grown-up children, so my function here is finished. I might as well die. The same would apply to your grandparents.

But science itself has a purpose! I am sure, when you write up a practical, you will start with the 'Aim' or a 'Prediction' or something, whatever your teacher has told you to do. You have a purpose in doing the practical – to find something out. Isn't that a bit weird? We have a purpose, which is to find out about something that has no purpose!

But maybe there are different ways of looking at the same thing. You know – looking from different angles. I get up in the morning and, being the almost perfect husband I am, I put the kettle[59] on to make my wife a cup of tea. My wife comes into the kitchen and asks, 'Why is the kettle boiling?' I can answer in two ways:

1. It's boiling because I switched the kettle on; that made an electrical connection and the flowing current caused the element to heat up; the heat has gone into the water which has in turn heated up and it has now reached 100°C which is the boiling point of water.

2. It's boiling because I want to make you a cup of tea.

---

[59] Image from https://openclipart.org/detail/243133/kettle (accessed 8th November 2017).

Which one is true? They are so different that, surely, they can't both be correct. Of course, you know they can both be correct. One is looking at cause; the other is looking at purpose. If my wife was interested in the science, then the first is the answer she was looking for; if she was wondering simply what I was trying to achieve, the second is correct. But if I give her the answer she is not looking for, it doesn't make my answer wrong, just not appropriate.

It's like that with science and faith. If I look at my function on earth scientifically, it is to reproduce my genes; if I look from most other angles, it could be all sorts of things – to pass on my knowledge or to glorify God, depending on what I mean by purpose.

As far as science is concerned, it is interested in function rather than purpose, but that doesn't mean there is no purpose. It just means we shouldn't include purpose in science. It's not appropriate. Science is limited in what it can tell you about the universe. It will always be limited because it can't tell why you are here. That doesn't mean science is lacking – it's just not supposed to investigate that sort of thing.

If we allow our lives to be ruled entirely by looking at function rather than purpose, we are liable to end up with a cold, grey, lifeless, joyless, colourless existence. Communism had, as one of its central pillars, an insistence on atheism and a functional scientific outlook. Communist countries ended up being the most dreary, colourless places you can imagine. They were entirely functional, and beauty disappeared out of the window. The soul went out of the people.

On the other hand, to ignore the science behind our lives is to be uncritical in our thoughts and allow all sorts of erroneous ways of thinking to creep in.

We need science and we also need to look beyond it to the wonderful purpose in human existence if we want to have a rounded and wholesome approach to life.

I don't care if your science teacher tells you science has got all the answers to everything in life. I hope they would not be so ignorant, but if they are, they are wrong. You have to understand life for yourself, not the way I understand it or your teacher or parents understand it, so don't just accept the opinions of others.

According to faith (well, at least Christian faith), everyone has a purpose, whether or not they realise it. You are not here for nothing, or just to live and then die. You are part of society and you can make a positive difference to other people's lives. Your grandparents may well be making a good contribution to your life. You can be certain virtually every scientist you ever meet will believe they have a purpose.

Even Richard Dawkins, who insists that purpose is a childish illusion, has a purpose in his writing. He says, 'If this book works as I intend [his purpose], religious readers who open it will be atheists when they put it down.'[60]

But we need to ask some questions.

Why bother with having a purpose in science? What's the advantage of discovering how the universe began? Why not just live life, produce some children, bring them up and then die? Why go through all the hassle of school,

---

[60] Dawkins, *The God Delusion*, p27.

university, tests, homework, exams and so on when none of it has any point?

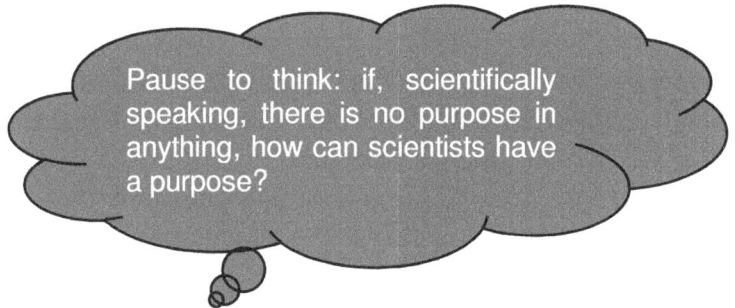

Pause to think: if, scientifically speaking, there is no purpose in anything, how can scientists have a purpose?

I reckon it all comes down to a few facts.

Science can answer (at least potentially) everything to do with processes. How this or that happens; how something works. It can explain masses of stuff. It is essential to our understanding. But it can't tell you everything.

It can't interpret a poem; it can't tell you definitely if your boyfriend or girlfriend truly loves you; it can't tell you what outfit to wear to a party, though it could be helpful for colour matching; it can't tell you that something is beautiful. It certainly can't tell you what your purpose in life is apart from the biology.

All those things are looking at life from a non-scientific angle. Remember 'non-scientific' does not mean 'unscientific'. If you want to go beyond scientific understanding, you need to look from other angles.

Faith says you have a purpose. Faith says the universe has a purpose. It was created for God and God created us to have creatures with whom to share His enjoyment. Scientists who study astrophysics do so because they find delight in their studies and exploration. We could say God is sharing His delight with them and loves their inquisitive attitude even though many do not acknowledge Him.

If you want to understand what faith is really about (not what atheists think it means), you need to look around the corner, as it were. The problem is, some people don't think there's a corner; they think the only things that are real are those we can see, touch or measure.

So, I would now like to try to give you some idea of what faith is about according to the Bible rather than what the atheists think it is about.

9. What Is Faith Really About?

Mark Twain wrote a book called *Following the Equator.* He was around back in the late nineteenth century. In this book, he said, 'Faith is believing what you know ain't so.'[61] Atheists love to quote that because that is exactly what they think it is. Search for Mark Twain and that quote on the internet and you'll find it on loads of atheist sites.

Richard Dawkins says (this is how he thinks Christians think):

> Faith (belief without evidence) is a virtue. The more your beliefs defy the evidence, the more virtuous you are. Virtuoso believers who can manage to believe something really weird, unsupported and insupportable, in the teeth of evidence and reason, are especially highly rewarded.[62]

---

[61] Mark Twain, *Following the Equator* (Public Domain Books), p70.
[62] Dawkins, *The God Delusion*, p231.

The late Christopher Hitchens (another famous atheist author) wrote:

> Faith is the surrender of the mind, it's the surrender of reason, it's the surrender of the only thing that makes us different from other animals. It's our need to believe and to surrender our skepticism and our reason, our yearning to discard that and put all our trust or faith in someone or something, that is the sinister thing to me ... Out of all the virtues, all the supposed virtues, faith must be the most overrated.[63]

Is this really what it is?

Compare what these three people said with what Galileo Galilei ('father of observational astronomy') said: 'I do not feel obliged to believe that the same God who has endowed

---

[63] http://www.goodreads.com/quotes/503115-faith-is-the-surrender-of-the-mind-it-is-the-surrender (accessed 10th September 2017).

us with senses, reason and intellect has intended us to forego their use.'[64]

It's clear that he saw the use of reason to be God-given and to be used sensibly – so faith and reason are linked together.

About my question above: No other animal believes in God (as far as we know), so to suggest that faith can make us no different from other mammals is ludicrous. I have to admit, though, that some people do surrender their reason when they say they believe the Bible, but faith is not surrendering your reason.

What does the Bible itself say about faith?

Obviously, the Bible has a huge amount to say about this subject, but there is what is considered a definition of faith in the Bible. It says, 'Now faith is the substance of things hoped for, the evidence of things not seen.'[65] The word for 'evidence' here, in the Greek (the language of the New Testament), is *elenchos*, which means proof, proving or testing. So, faith is testing things out; things that are unseen. It has to work. Does that sound anything like what the three learned gentlemen above said? It certainly doesn't to me!

Faith needs evidence; it is not believing against the evidence. Mark Twain, Richard Dawkins and Christopher Hitchens have got this bit totally wrong. They thought they

---

[64] http://www.huffingtonpost.com/entry/12-famous-scientists-on-the-possibility-of-god_us_56afa292e4b057d7d7c7a1e5 (accessed 10th September 2017).

[65] Hebrews 11:1 (KJV).

knew or think they know what faith is but, in reality, they haven't a clue. I look forward to atheists, none of whom has any clue about faith, stopping pretending they do and criticising things they know nothing about.

By the way, I also look forward to those Christians who know little about science but who pretend they do, stopping and admitting they don't have the answers. Perhaps we'd then be able to listen to each other and learn something valuable!

In the next chapter, I will examine the kind of evidence we are talking about in faith. But let me say this first.

Faith in science

You have to have faith to do science. You must believe you can find the answers (but you may not). You must be prepared to fail before you succeed and, like Thomas Edison[66] trying to produce a workable light bulb, you may fail 1,000 times. Aren't you glad he didn't give up? Basically, you must believe before you get the evidence on occasions.

But how about scientific facts? How about things that are already proved? Well, science is littered with laws and theories that we all believed were true for all time but have now been found to be false, or only to be true under certain

---

[66] Image from https://wpclipart.com/famous/inventors/Edison/Thomas_Edison_sketch.png.html (accessed 11th November 2017).

circumstances, such as Newton's[67] laws of motion. So, we have to take everything we believe on some kind of faith, but it's the kind of faith that says, 'If the evidence is found to disprove this, I will change my belief.'

So, we have two kinds of faith in science: (1) the faith that pushes the boundaries and believes answers can be found and (2) the faith that believes things that have already been discovered, even though they may be shown to be incorrect in the future. Both of those require evidence. I believe new things can be discovered because of past evidence that we are continually discovering new things. I believe certain 'facts' because I trust the evidence that people have uncovered to prove the facts.

On the first type of faith, I may believe a wonder cure for cancer will be discovered by the end of next year because researchers are making excellent progress. I may be right or wrong. I will only discover at the end of next year, but right now I believe it by faith on certain evidence. If nobody had faith that a cure for cancer could be found, no one would work on finding one.

On the second type of faith, I may believe that all living things are composed of cells because that is what the evidence tells me. I may be right or wrong. I have to understand that I could be wrong. It is possible that some living thing not composed of cells may be discovered. I will

[67] Image from https://wpclipart.com/famous/science/Newton/Isa ac_Newton_drawing.png.html (11th November 2017).

only know if that happens but meanwhile, I accept on faith that Cell Theory is true.

Faith in God may not be the same as faith in science, but there are clear similarities, as we will see. Evidence for believing in God is more like evidence in a court of law rather than scientific evidence.

10. Surely Seeing Is Believing – and I Can't See Him?

If we are looking at faith from the point of view of the Bible, it would make sense to see what the Bible says about it. We've already seen that what some atheists say about faith is nonsense.

We've seen what the Bible says faith is; now here's a description. It says, 'And without faith it is impossible to please him, for whoever would draw near to God must believe that he exists and that he rewards those who seek him.'[68]

There are three things here:

1. Real faith pleases God.

2. If you want to approach Him, you need to believe He is there.

3. He rewards those who genuinely seek Him.

---

[68] Hebrews 11:6 (ESV).

You may have heard people say that you need to have childlike faith. They are quoting Jesus, who said, 'Truly, I say to you, whoever does not receive the kingdom of God like a child shall not enter it.'[69]

You may have been told that means you should not question what the Bible says, but just trust it and believe it no matter what it says. But is that right?

Firstly, what does it mean to believe the Bible? Does it mean I have to believe it literally? To some, that would be it. And where in the Bible does it say that believing the Bible is a definition of faith or that it means I have received the kingdom? It doesn't.

My experience of small children is that they are full of questions and wonder. Yes, they may be gullible, but they are full of curiosity. Could it be that Jesus was talking about having an attitude that says 'I don't know the answers but I really want to know'? He certainly didn't mean childish faith and I'm sure He didn't mean us to be gullible.

I am not going to go into the first point I mentioned but, in this chapter, I will look at believing that God is there (point 2). In the next chapter, I'll look at point 3 – about faith in action – the kind of faith where God rewards those who seek Him by answering prayer.

Believing He is there

I battled over this one as a teenager. What is He? Where is He? Where is heaven? What is God like? Science gave me evidence and seeing was believing. But I couldn't see God and had no clue even where to look. There didn't seem to

---

[69] Luke 18:17 (ESV).

be any evidence. I prayed especially when we needed rain badly on our farm, but my prayers didn't appear to make any difference.

Let me try (as best I can) to say what I have found in answer to some of these questions.

God doesn't need anything for His existence

The Bible never actually says that God exists. It just says He is. You find this in the first three chapters of the book of Exodus – the story of Moses meeting God in the desert. Moses was born to a Hebrew family when the Hebrews were slaves in Egypt in the second millennium BC.

The Egyptians were cruel to them big-time but were also scared that they would rebel, so they decided to get rid of all male Hebrew children. They commanded the Hebrews to kill them at birth. Talk about child abuse!

Understandably, the Hebrew mothers didn't all obey, and neither did the midwives. Moses' mother was one of them. She hid her precious baby in a basket among the bulrushes on the Nile[70] (I would have been worried about the crocodiles).

Anyway, one of the Egyptian princesses found him and thought, 'Ahhh.' She had to keep him! He ended up being brought up as a prince but always knew he was actually a Hebrew. One day, he found an Egyptian beating up a

---

[70] Image from https://www.pdclipart.org/displayimage.php?alb um=98&pos=10 (accessed 10th November 2017).

Hebrew, so, like you do, he killed the Egyptian. But he got found out.

To cut a long story short, he had to flee to the desert to avoid getting his just deserts. (Sorry, I couldn't resist that one!)

He was there for ages and one day he saw a bush on fire.[71] This wasn't unusual,[72] but this time the bush wasn't burning up. So, he went to have a look – well, you probably would, too.

Now, just to get scientific for a moment: what does fire (combustion) need?

It needs (1) fuel, (2) oxygen and (3) something to trigger it. You've learned that in the 'fire triangle' but I don't think Moses knew the science of combustion, so he probably didn't get the message completely, though I'm sure he knew you couldn't have a fire without something to burn.

It seems as if this fire wasn't using up the fuel (the bush), so it probably wasn't using any oxygen either.

When Moses got there, God spoke to him. That must have been pretty shocking. Moses ended up asking God His name and He said it was 'I AM'.[73] If anyone else gave their name as 'I am', it would not be very helpful.

But what it seems was happening is that God appeared as a fire (a talking fire – no wonder Moses was surprised).

---

[71] Image from https://openclipart.org/detail/269013/07-exodus-41017-01 (accessed 8th November 2017).

[72] In the desert, morning dew drops can cause the sun's rays to focus on a dry twig and set it on fire.

[73] Exodus 3:14 (ESV).

But this fire didn't need anything else for its existence. It didn't need fuel or oxygen. It was separate from the creation. It just WAS. God just IS; that's why He said His name was 'I AM'.

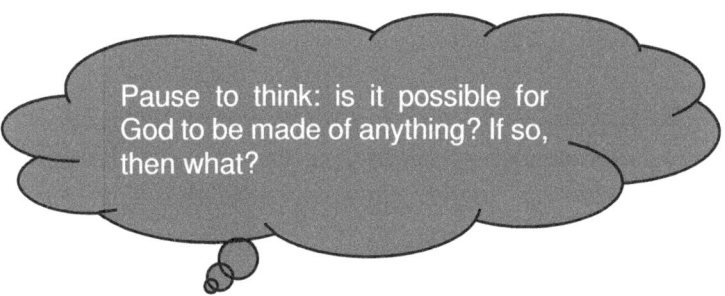

Pause to think: is it possible for God to be made of anything? If so, then what?

OK, so what's that about?

This is really important. What this story tells us is that God is not part of the universe. You can search every nook and cranny; every crook and nanny; every supernova, every black hole, every galaxy, every atom, every proton and photon, but you will never find God. Why? Because He is not part of the universe. God doesn't exist scientifically. Maybe that's amazing coming from someone who calls himself a Christian. But it's true.

God doesn't exist in the way we think of existence – you know, made of matter or energy or something.

King Solomon built the temple that his father, King David, had planned to build. He prayed to God at its dedication. His prayer is found in the first book of Kings, chapter 8, and the second book of Chronicles, chapter 6. He asked God to specially bless this building and listen to the prayers made in it. He was asking God to live there but he went on:

> But will God indeed dwell with man on the earth? Behold, heaven and the highest heaven cannot contain you, how much less this house that I have built![74]

The heaven in this case is simply the universe. He was saying God can't be contained in the universe. He is not 'somewhere up there'. He's outside the universe – completely different from it.

And that is exactly where the New Atheists go wrong. They think it is a scientific question. Well, it's not. They think if there is a God, He must be somewhere in the universe. That's nonsense. Science can only investigate what's in the universe, and God isn't. The kind of God they attack doesn't exist anyway, but that's not the God the Bible is talking about. There is absolutely no point in attacking someone's belief if you've got the belief wrong in the first place.

There's more to it than this, of course, but Christians believe in this God. A God who is 'transcendent'. Now there's a complicated word for you. What does it mean? Just that He is completely separate from ('other than') the universe.

---

[74] 2 Chronicles 6:18 (ESV).

But hang on a moment

I thought God was supposed to create all things? How can He do that if He is so separate from the universe? How could He speak to people if He is completely outside the universe? He'd have to shout pretty loudly!

He gets everywhere

King David, in Psalm 139, asks where he can go to hide from God's presence and says, wherever he might try to hide, God is there. There was also this bloke who lived in the land of Israel more than 2,500 years ago (a bit before computers and mobile phones but later than dinosaurs) called Jeremiah. He was called a prophet and the New Testament tells us that God spoke by the prophets.[75] One time he was telling people they couldn't hide away from God and he quoted what God said to him. He said, 'Do I not fill heaven and earth?'[76] So, Christians (and Jews, by the way) believe that God is absolutely everywhere. Because 'fill' really does mean fill.

So, on the one hand He's nowhere to be found, and on the other hand He is everywhere. Maybe you're thinking, 'Make up your mind. Which is it?'

Well, if He is not part of the universe, we will never find Him in a scientific way, but because of that, He can be everywhere all at the same time. The theological word for that is 'immanent'. That's where we get 'Immanuel' from – the name I mentioned in chapter 4. He is present

---

[75] Hebrews 1:1.
[76] Jeremiah 23:24 (ESV).

everywhere all the time. We cannot see Him or discover Him with our normal five senses, by any instrument now or in the future, or by our brains alone. But that doesn't mean He isn't there. Christians claim to have discovered Him or to have 'found' Him. It is probably truer to say He has found them.

One other point on this: if you think about it, if He was to be found somewhere in the universe, it would be impossible for Him to be everywhere. If He is infinite, as Christians believe, then it is possible for Him to be everywhere. If He could be seen and He was everywhere, would we be able to see anything else?

Nothing I've said gives evidence that this is true, but it shows that we can't look at scientific evidence to prove or disprove God. We will have to look at other types of evidence for that.

But, before we do that, I want to look at a more important part of faith – faith in action. You only do what you really believe, so saying you believe something and then not acting according to your belief actually means you don't really believe it.

11. Faith in Action

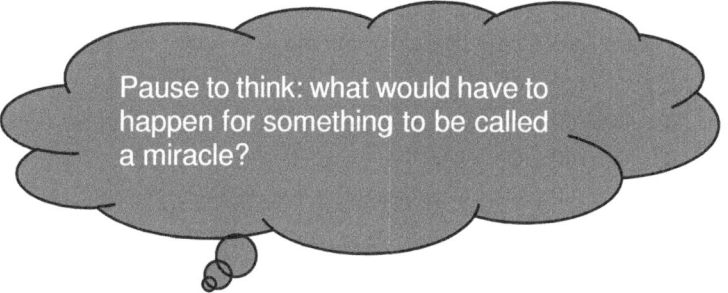

Pause to think: what would have to happen for something to be called a miracle?

I think most people reading this would be incredibly surprised at some of the things that happen as a result of Christians having faith in God's ability to do active things in life. You may think it's all about attending 'church services' but that's only a small part of it.

The apostle James said something that worries a lot of Christians. He said:

> What good is it, my brothers, if someone says he has faith but does not have works? Can that faith save him? … faith by itself, if it does not have works, is dead. But someone will say, 'You have faith and I have works. Show me your faith apart from your works, and I will show you my faith by my works.' You believe that God is one; you

do well. Even the demons believe – and shudder![77]

You see, a Bible kind of faith means that just believing God is there is all very well, but it means nothing unless it results in action. It's in action that your faith is tested to see if it is real.

Without action it's, I suppose, a bit like starving with hunger and believing that the food in front of you will stop your starvation, but then not eating the food. Stupid? Yes, of course, but that's how a few Christians behave!

Atheists think faith is only to do with believing God exists and nothing else.

But, did you know, there are Christians who have been or are involved in all sorts of social action, such as:

- abolishing slavery; not just in the nineteenth century, but they are acting today to try to stop trafficking of children and women for the sex trade;

- abolishing the workhouses that existed in Britain;

- helping women with pregnancy crises; post-abortion work and so on;

- reaching out to the poorest people in the world and empowering them.

That is a tiny list among thousands of things done by Christians worldwide. However, that's probably what you

---

[77] James 2:14, 17-19 (ESV).

would expect, and there are non-Christians who do a lot of good things, too, including what I have mentioned above.

Did you know, though, that across the world every single day, people are healed from some terrible diseases and conditions through Christians praying for them?

- there have been people raised from the dead (probably only a few a year);[78]

- blind people suddenly receive their sight;

- deaf people are suddenly able to hear;

- legs and arms that are too short are lengthened;

- cancers are healed.

Again, that is just a tiny list out of the array of healings that take place.

Now, I imagine you may well think that is impossible. He's making it up. How does he know? Well, I'll tell you how I know. Apart from raising the dead (and there are lots of cases of that you can look up on the internet), I have seen all the others happen. I have seen blind people get their sight, deaf people suddenly hearing, legs and arms suddenly lengthening, someone's back healed when she had metal rods down the backbone – she could suddenly touch her toes, cancers healed . . .

A well-known case of amazing healing is that of Howard Storm. I'm not sure if he actually died, but he

---

[78] Check this site out for documented cases:
http://documentedhealings.com/category/raised-from-death-2/
(accessed 8th October 2017),

certainly had a shocking near-death experience and turned from an atheist to a believer, and later a Christian pastor.[79] I came across a documented case of a doctor, Sean George, who was raised from the dead in 2008 after fifty-five minutes and was perfectly all right.[80] An evangelist, Reinhard Bonnke, preaches to crowds in Africa and has seen people raised from the dead.[81] This next link tells you the story of the first time an African preacher, Surprise Sithole, experienced someone being raised from the dead.[82]

All the cases I have seen were genuine healings and they happened without medicine. I have also seen people healed of cancer when they were being treated medically but were not expected to live at all.

What I have experienced is nothing compared with what you can read about on the websites I have included in the footnotes in this chapter, but I can tell you a few stories of when I have prayed and seen people instantly healed and when He has amazingly supplied me with what I need. I mention these not because I am anything special, but because they are first-hand experiences. Let me start with when He has supplied me with my needs.

---

[79] http://blog.godreports.com/2012/03/atheist-professors-near-death-experience-in-hell-left-him-changed/ (accessed 14th October 2017).
[80] http://sheridanvoysey.com/Miracle-Sean-George-Raised-From-Dead (accessed 14th October 2017).
[81] https://www.youtube.com/watch?v=BY7wTz0mw24 (accessed 20th October 2017).
[82] https://www.youtube.com/watch?v=du094cmVKI0 (accessed 1st November 2017).

Holey underpants

I'm going to let you into a secret. At university, I was very poor. My underpants were not in good condition. The holes got worse and worse with time. My landlady, bless her, tried to repair them, but it was hopeless. She said, 'You really need to buy some new underpants.'

But I could hardly afford my food, so I replied (all casual-like), 'The Lord will provide!'

She said, 'You can't say the Lord will provide. You have to buy some.'

Now, I must say I didn't spend a lot of time praying for underpants, but God knew I needed them. You can't pretend with Him and He knew what my underpants were like, even though no one else did (apart from my landlady).

One Friday evening, a friend and I felt God was telling us to go into town and talk to people about Him. We hitch-hiked in and went into a coffee bar, but weren't able to talk to anyone. So, we started to walk back to the road going out to the university.

As we went along, a very drunk man came towards us. We ended up talking to him. It turned out he wanted to commit suicide. He said he was a psychiatrist and that he had helped others but couldn't help himself. He was an alcoholic. We said we would go back to his place with him. He was staying in a hotel room.

We talked to him till 2am, then put him to bed, saying we would see him in the morning. We hitch-hiked back and then returned by 8am.

He was now sober and we talked to him for hours while he attacked what we were saying. He really was a psychiatrist! I thought I was making a complete pig's ear of my answers but after a couple of hours, he said, 'I've attacked you in every way I can; I like what you've got and I want it.' I was amazed.

Anyway, he was lying on the bed and suddenly said, 'Excuse the state of my socks!' They had holes in them. I said, 'That's OK, you want to see the state of my underpants!'

So he said, 'I've just bought a pack of new ones. I'll give them to you!'

'I can't take your underpants,' I replied.

'Why not?' he said. 'You've helped me; I want to help you.'

So, I thanked him very much, took the packet of three new pairs of underpants, plonked them on the table at home and said to my landlady, 'The Lord has provided!' She never ever forgot that!

Other times we have been helped

I'm not going to tell you all the stories of how God has provided for what we need as a family, but several times we have had exactly the right amount of money at exactly the right time when we had absolutely nothing left, because we prayed about our situation. After I left Bible college in 1981, I worked in a church in London as an assistant pastor and supervisor of a small school in the church building. I was on a very low wage and there were times when we literally had no money to buy food for our supper and someone knocked on the door and gave us a cooked meal on a tray. I'm not joking. These things happened.

Am I saying that in these cases God appeared and provided us with our needs? Of course not. It was people who did it. This could all be coincidence. But it is amazing how many times we have been provided with exactly what we needed at exactly the right time and in answer to prayer. We interpret it as God's provision.

Can God use ordinary people to heal?

I truly am very ordinary. I am not a 'spiritual healer', whatever that is. I'm just a normal person. Well, I hope I am! God uses ordinary people. What I will tell you now is the sort of thing that happens with thousands of Christians around the world, and loads of them experience far more amazing things than this. The only reason I'm telling you what has happened with me is that I have seen it happen in front of my own eyes and, if I am so ordinary, it means it could happen with you, if you have faith.

When we were in London, we had a man in the church with terrible arthritis in his knees. The only thing left for the doctors to do was to remove his kneecaps, scrape the crystals off his knee joints, and put the kneecaps back.

I was leading the meeting one Sunday evening when he prayed and thanked God for his pain. I felt for him and prayed out loud for his healing, hoping he would feel a bit less pain. Suddenly all the pain left and he ran around the building, arms in the air, tears running down his face, saying over and over, 'Thank You, Jesus!'

He went to the doctor the next day; the doctor wouldn't believe that God could have healed him, but when he went back about a month later, all the crystals had gone! I asked another doctor if that could happen. He said the pain can come and go, but the crystals do not just disappear. Was that a miracle? I don't know.

A while later, after we had moved to Glastonbury, my wife was suffering from terrible back pain. She said she wondered if one leg was shorter than the other. I thought, 'Oh no! That means I will have to pray and I really can't believe God could lengthen her leg using me', even though I had seen it happen with other people.

We checked her leg carefully and the right was about an inch shorter than the left. With her backside right up against the back of the chair and holding her legs out carefully, I closed my eyes because I didn't dare look, and prayed. I said, 'Lord, you know I haven't got faith for this, but it's over to You. Please equalise her legs.' I felt a movement; she said, 'Something's happened.' We looked and her legs were the same length!

Now it was actually a joint going back (the sacroiliac joint), but it happened totally silently. Over the next year or so, it went out again a few times but every time we prayed, it immediately went back.

I prayed for other people who had back problems because of their legs, and every one of them was healed. One young lady had been to the doctor who said the only thing they could do was to cut an inch or so out of her longer leg. She was not a Christian but I said to her, 'You don't need to do that; God can heal you.' After checking her legs again, I prayed and her leg grew in front of my eyes. That was not a joint going back. Her leg literally grew in a couple of seconds. Was that a miracle? I will leave you to decide what you think. But I can guarantee it happened. Her dance teacher immediately noticed the difference.

What's the likelihood of that happening without medicine, or even with medicine? If it wasn't God, then what was it? Positive thinking? I don't think so. She was not expecting anything to happen, and I've never known positive thinking to cause a leg to grow an inch in a second or so.

What is this kind of faith?

You may think faith that sees people being healed is for special people – the 'saints' that we hear of in the Roman Catholic or Anglican churches. Well, it's not. It's for every Christian. As far as the Church in the first century was concerned, all believers were saints, and are called that in the Bible. The apostle Paul (the Bible never calls him 'Saint Paul') often called the believers in a town or region the 'saints'[83] even though he then ticked some of them off big-time. And that is actually still true today – nothing's changed. A saint is not someone who is above others in the holiness stakes. A saint is anyone who genuinely believes in Christ and follows Him.

But praying for healing is not guaranteed to work every time. At least to start with, it probably fails far more often than it works. It may not be because we've prayed wrongly; it may be because God doesn't always answer the way we think He should, or possibly He wants us to learn a more important lesson through it. It's definitely not some sort of success formula.

---

[83] Romans 1:7; 1 Corinthians 1:2; Ephesians 1:1; Philippians 1:1; Colossians 1:2.

But it's the kind of faith that says, 'God has promised to heal us, so I will pray; it may not work, but I will learn from my mistakes and keep on till I find it working, and I will get to know God more in the process.'

It's a faith that grows and changes with time. It's something like the scientist who believes they will find the answer to a problem and persists till it works.

The reason I became more confident to pray for the lady who had a leg shorter than the other was because I had seen evidence beforehand of people's legs being lengthened when I prayed for them. When I first prayed for my wife's legs, I knew it *could* happen because I had seen others praying for limbs to be lengthened and it had worked; I just had doubts that it would happen when I prayed, but I was prepared to risk it not working.

As I write this, my wife, Lizzie, is having regular scans for a possible melanoma. A melanoma is a very dangerous kind of skin cancer. She had one on her leg in 2015. They operated to remove it and then tried a further operation to get to the base, but that was unsuccessful. She was referred to The Royal Marsden Hospital in London where she was to have an 'isolated limb perfusion' – a dangerous procedure that could kill her. Before this, three more tumours grew on her leg. She was due to have the procedure done in April 2016 but when she arrived, they found the three tumours had disappeared completely. She had another operation to remove one in her groin but now, in October 2017, she has had no further cancers.

The surgeons cannot understand how these tumours disappeared. In fact, we have literally just returned from an appointment with the surgeon. He said he thought this needed to be written up in a medical journal and his comment was, 'Whoever you are talking to, keep on talking!' It had never happened before. A lot of people were praying for her. I am not going to say either that this was a miracle or that she is completely healed because we don't know what lies in the future, but something very strange and inexplicable happened. Was it God? I will leave that to your opinion.

My trust in God grows all the time I am prepared to risk something; maybe risk looking stupid if it doesn't work.

I am prepared to look stupid because I have faith that God loves me and accepts me anyway, and it doesn't really matter what other people think of me. They can think I am stupid, but that is just their opinion, and if God doesn't agree with them, then they are disagreeing with Him. Am I bothered?

It takes time for faith like that to grow. Faith changes all the time (it's dynamic). It's not static, as atheists would have you believe. It's always pushing the boundaries. Faith is not just about believing certain things you are told. It's about trusting a God of love, stepping out in that trust, and acting on it.

Remember part of the description of faith was that it 'is the substance of things hoped for'.[84] That means it is real, not just hoping against hope. It makes what we hope for become real.

Is faith all to do with action? Is it all about miracles? Absolutely not. In fact, it's to do with character as well. It's not just what we do; it's also what we are like as people.

---

[84] Hebrews 11:1 (KJV).

Let's have a look now at how people who have faith change.

12. The Fruit of Faith

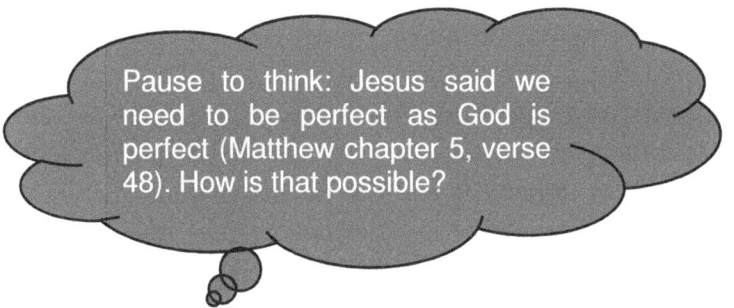

Pause to think: Jesus said we need to be perfect as God is perfect (Matthew chapter 5, verse 48). How is that possible?

At school, when learning about religions, you generally learn about their beliefs, discuss their moral codes and things like that. That's all fine and OK, but it's not really what Christianity is about at all.

The whole thing about living a Christian life is that you can't!

Now, you're going to think I'm bonkers. What on earth is the point of it if you can't live it? Jesus, before He departed, told His disciples that He was sending 'another Comforter'[85] – i.e. a Comforter like Himself. By the way, 'Comforter' does not mean someone who pats your back and says, 'There, there, I'm sure everything will be all

---

[85] John 14:16 (KJV).

right!' when you've just failed an exam. It means someone who stands with you all the time and strengthens you, sometimes having to convince you that you can do things you don't think you can!

He was talking about the Holy Spirit. The Holy Spirit is God Himself, not some force blowing from on high, or an impersonal fire, or anything else. Living a Christian life is actually to do with having a personal relationship with God with His Spirit living in you. He strengthens you and helps you to live the life He wants; you can't do it on your own at all.

You can make New Year's resolutions with the best intentions; you can battle to keep the Ten Commandments; you can try as hard as you can to live up to the standards Jesus set; you can do your level best to 'love the Lord your God and love your neighbour as yourself'. You will fail. You can't do it. No one can! Unfortunately, millions of Christians across the world think they have to battle to be good; they try and fail, feel a failure, and many give up.

Only the Holy Spirit, living in you, can do it in you. It's not easy admitting you can't do it; it makes you think you're useless (if you don't understand this). It takes humility. Most people find that really hard. I have never known this important Christian teaching to be taught in schools. How would you teach it? It's nothing to do with passing exams.

The fruit of the Spirit[86]

The Fruit of the spirit
Galatians 5:22-23

When the apostle Paul wrote to the Christians in Galatia, he was trying to show them that living by their own efforts to be good (the Law) was useless and that they needed the Holy Spirit. He said that the Holy Spirit produced certain characteristics in people. He called this the 'fruit of the Spirit'. This 'fruit' consists of 'love, joy, peace, patience, kindness, goodness, faithfulness, gentleness, self-control'.[87]

Another thing Paul tells us is that faith does not come from us. I can't decide to have faith. Deciding to believe the Bible does not give me faith, though a number of Christians think it does. Paul tells us faith is given us by God:

> For by grace you have been saved through faith. And this is not your own doing; it is the gift of God.[88]

I am sure there are loads of people who would call themselves Christians, maybe because:

- they have been baptised as a baby and confirmed later, or

- they attend church meetings, or

---

[86] Image from http://www.clker.com/cliparts/2/l/d/P/f/a/the-fruit-of-the-spirit-md.png (accessed 11th November 2017).
[87] Galatians 5:22-23.
[88] Ephesians 2:8 (ESV).

- their parents are Christians, or

- they believe God exists, or even

- they think they live a good enough life.

But none of these makes you a Christian. The Bible says it is people who were born 'not of blood' (because their parents are Christians), 'nor of the will of the flesh' (their own efforts), 'nor of the will of man' (because someone wants you to be a Christian), 'but of God'.[89]

The way God deals with us is through His Spirit, so it is the Holy Spirit who gives us faith. Although there is a decision from a person themselves in becoming a Christian, strictly speaking God is the one who gives us faith. How can you know it has happened? Well, you find your whole attitude to life changes; suddenly God is the centre, not you; you find yourself loving Him when previously you didn't really care, even if you did believe in His existence.

Faith produces right-living, kind but courageous, loving people who are secure and considerate of others, seeking the good of other people. It makes people able to get on with others and have a joyful manner.

Knowing that God is with you and is not condemning you for your sins and mess-ups; knowing that He is on your side and is with you all the time means you can grow in confidence because your confidence is based on His power, not your own.

---

[89] John 1:13 (ESV).

112

I'm sure you'll be able to say you know Christians who are not like that at all.

You're probably right. Some Christians are miserable, but you can't blame faith for that. It's because they are not exercising faith, rather than that faith makes them like that.

And, actually, no Christian is perfect. Every Christian is what could be called a 'work in progress'. As we learn to exercise faith more, as we understand God more, so we slowly get closer to what He wants, because the Holy Spirit transforms people from the inside out.

OK. Now, if living like this is impossible without the Holy Spirit, what does that say about faith and the existence of God? You've been waiting patiently for this evidence! Let's look at the next chapter.

13. Is There Any Proof of God?

I have said all along that we can't prove God exists. Some people decide they will believe 'just in case', as if God would be fooled by such an insincere attitude. No, that won't do. Any atheist will tell you, you can't prove God. And they are right. Some will tell you that you need to choose between science and faith/religion; that this is where the disagreement is. And they are wrong.

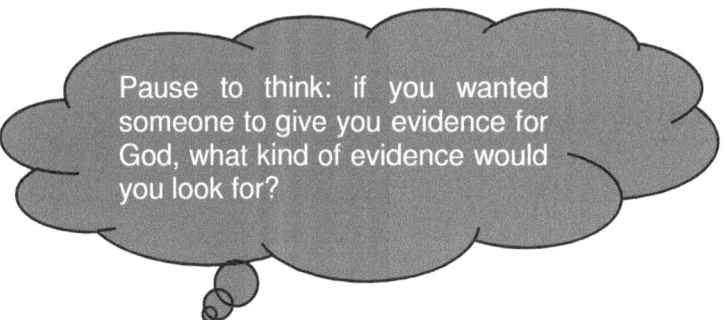

Pause to think: if you wanted someone to give you evidence for God, what kind of evidence would you look for?

Science is based on evidence or at least trying to find evidence that will 'prove' something to be right or wrong, but I hope I've shown that it's far more than that. A biblical kind of faith is about exploring and risking making mistakes. It's about having lives transformed for the better.

Atheists will tell you that faith is not based on evidence at all. That, I hope you have seen, is rubbish.

Faith needs evidence. I don't believe something because somebody tells me something, however much I may think of them. I must also be careful of my own interpretations of the Bible. I keep on finding I've misunderstood things, or that there is another angle I never thought of before. So why do I believe it? Well, if faith produces what I have described in previous chapters, we would expect to see evidence of it happening in people who have faith.

If the effects of knowing God as described in the Bible turn out to be practically true in my life, and in the lives of others, that is evidence that it works. If I find amazing ways in which the teaching in the Bible is true to life, especially modern life thousands of years after it was written, that is evidence that it has lasting wisdom. If I find that people really do get set free from the negative things in their lives – things such as depression, sickness and so on – then that is evidence that faith works. If I find quite staggering answers to prayer, for example some of the healings I mentioned earlier, then that is evidence that someone/something answering to God's description is at work.

You see, truly being a Christian means having your life transformed - maybe not in a blinding flash, but certainly transformed – changed for the better. And not just when you first believe, but every year, every month, every week and every day you are being changed little by little into someone more like Jesus.

If you are a Christian and you never change like that, I suggest you question whether you have ever really given your life to Him. There are plenty of people who claim to be Christians but are not. You can't transform a Ford Fiesta into a Rolls-Royce by driving it into a Rolls-Royce factory. And you can't turn into a Christian just by 'going to church' or by being baptised or confirmed or by trying to be good.

Professor Andrew Sims, who was president of the Royal College of Psychiatrists from 1990 to 1993, wrote a book, *Is Faith Delusion?* In it, he speaks about a massive study done by Koenig, McCullough and Larson that was published in 2001 on the effects of religious involvement on health. This study was done by examining more than 1,600 other studies which were mainly carried out on Christians, but also a few on Jewish people and other religions. Their comment was:

> In the majority of studies, religious involvement is correlated with well-being, happiness and life satisfaction; hope and optimism; purpose and meaning in life; higher self-esteem; better adaptation to bereavement; greater social support and less loneliness; lower rates of depression; lower rates of suicide and fewer positive attitudes towards suicide; less anxiety; less psychosis and fewer psychotic tendencies; lower rates of alcohol and drug abuse; less delinquency and criminal activity; greater marital stability and satisfaction … We concluded that, for the vast majority of people,

the apparent benefit of devout religious belief and practice probably outweigh the risks.[90]

The risks they mention are mainly that some believers do not consult medical professionals when they should do. Sims says that even though the authors were cautious in their conclusions, the results were overwhelming. In his book, he says one of the best-kept secrets of the psychiatric profession is that those who participate regularly in worship receive distinct health benefits. He reckons that if the results had shown the opposite, it would have made headline news and Richard Dawkins certainly would have commented on it to show that faith had a negative effect.

That, of course, is not direct evidence for the existence of God, but it is evidence that faith works.

None of this transformation stuff I have mentioned can be used as *proof* of God, but the fact that countless millions of people all over the world have experienced that transformation and there are thousands upon thousands more each day who start being transformed[91] is extremely strong evidence that God or someone or something just like Him does exist.

One or two 'miraculous' healings that cannot be explained by medicine may be simple coincidence, but if thousands are happening every day around the world, as I am sure is occurring, that can't be explained as

---

[90] Andrew Sims, *Is Faith Delusion?* (London: Continuum, 2009), p100, quoting from Koenig, McCullough & Larson, *Handbook of Religion and Health*.

[91] http://www.thetravelingteam.org/articles/growth-of-the-church (accessed 23rd December 2017).

coincidence, especially when they are all so closely linked with prayer. The fact that so many of those healings are linked with particular people who have dared to step out and act on faith would prompt any reasonable person to open their minds to see if, just maybe, God is at work! A dyed-in-the-wool atheist would say that if there is any chance at all (however tiny) of something 'just happening', they would rather go for that than think there might be a God.

One way that could be used to investigate whether faith or prayer has an effect would be to work out the statistical significance of the number of 'miracles' taking place associated with prayer compared with the number happening without any prayer.

In a court of law,[92] the person accused is usually found guilty or not guilty not because of absolute scientific proof, but because the weight of evidence is strong enough to be considered 'proof' that they did or didn't do it. What I have mentioned above is a similar type of evidence.

Another piece of strong evidence of God is Jesus Christ, but we will look at that evidence in the next chapter.

---

[92] Image from https://openclipart.org/detail/277740/justice-scales-silhouette (accessed 28th November 2017.

14. If God Does Exist, Then What Is He Like?

This is tricky! How do you describe something that is outside the universe, something that doesn't exist in any way that we know existence? It's even harder than trying to explain to a baby in the womb about life in the world outside. Just imagine for a moment how you would do that! It would be much easier to wait till the baby was born and let them gradually find out for themselves.

Well, you know what? Jesus said that becoming a Christian was like being born. He called it being 'born again'. And He said that unless you are born again, you'll never understand the kingdom of God or anything to do with it. It's not to do with intelligence, or having a degree, or being especially religious. Something pretty major needs to happen to you!

Nic the vic

There was this highly religious leader (sort of like a vicar, I suppose) called Nicodemus (we'll call him 'Nic') who came to Jesus late at night so none of the other leaders would see him. He was trying to work out who this man was. Nic said to Him:

> Rabbi, we all know you're a teacher straight from God. No one could do all the God-pointing, God-revealing acts you do if God weren't in on it.[93]

Jesus, who often said things to wind people up and get them going with difficult statements, said:

> You're absolutely right. Take it from me: Unless a person is born from above, it's not possible to see what I'm pointing to – to God's kingdom.[94]

Nic got a bit wound up! He asked:

> How can anyone … be born who has already been born and grown up? You can't re-enter your mother's womb and be born again. What are you saying with all this 'born-from above' talk?[95]

To paraphrase Jesus' reply, He answered Nic:

> I'm talking about a different kind of birth. Yes, you need to be born naturally but also supernaturally (born of the Spirit). Otherwise you haven't a hope of understanding what I'm on about. It's a bit like the wind – you know it's blowing because you see the trees moving but you don't know where it comes from or where it

---

[93] John 3:2 (MSG).
[94] John 3:3 (MSG).
[95] John 3:4 (MSG).

goes. You can see the difference with people who are born of the Spirit of God, but you can't make out where they're coming from or understand what makes them what they are.[96]

That was typical – He didn't really give him an answer. He just provoked him to go and find out more – not in textbooks but by being around Jesus and learning from Him.

You see, even the disciples didn't know that Jesus was showing them what God was like. Jesus was a man (totally) but His whole character and way of life was demonstrating God to them. Because somehow (no one can fully explain how), this God who is not part of the universe became part of the universe when He became a man (Jesus Christ). But He still remained not part of the universe. Oh, my mind is beginning to boggle!

God is infinite and eternal

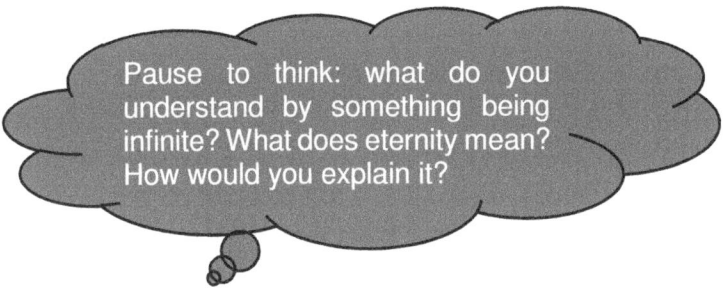

---

[96] John 3:5-8 (my paraphrase).

 You should have come across infinity[97] in maths. If you divide any number by zero, you get an error on the calculator – that's because it's infinity. It's an impossible number – you can't have anything larger.

So, how can anything be infinite?

I can't really understand infinity (I bet you can't either), but God is infinite. That doesn't mean He's a number bigger than any other. It means wherever He is, He is infinite. If we could see Him or if He was made of something, He wouldn't be infinite. So, He can be with you and with everyone else all over the world at the same time as well as being at the outer edges of the universe and outside it – even though we can't work out an 'outside' of the universe.

He is also eternal. Eternal doesn't just mean a very long time or even forever; it doesn't just mean never stopping. It means that as God is outside the universe, He is also outside time. He's not part of time; He doesn't exist in time. He can be at any time He wants, past, present and future all at the same time. Oh no, this is beginning to blow my mind! Fortunately, that would be a fairly minor explosion!

Don't worry if this is beyond you – it's beyond most people. I have some sort of vague grasp of what it's about. But if you haven't been born again, there's no hope of understanding it. Something has to change. In Jesus'

---

[97] Image from https://openclipart.org/detail/267822/infinity-arrow (accessed 11th November 2017).

words, 'You must be born again.'[98] No atheist can understand it – they would just think it was stupid.

But after all this complicated stuff, it boils down to this: the disciple Philip said to Jesus, 'Master, show us the Father; then we'll be content.'[99] Lots of people say things like, 'If God is there, why doesn't He show Himself to us?' Well, Jesus replied:

> You've been with me all this time, Philip, and you still don't understand? To see me is to see the Father.[100]

You may remember, when I tried to describe what God is, that I mentioned Moses meeting God in the form of a fire in the desert and that when Moses asked Him His name, He said His name was 'I AM'.[101] Well, Jesus used that name about Himself when the Jews asked Him if He had seen Abraham and He replied, 'Truly, truly, I say to you, before Abraham was, I am.'[102] That was considered the most holy name of God and the Jews were so offended, they wanted to stone Him.

In a way we cannot really understand, this God has shown Himself to us by becoming human. I suppose we can say He stepped into His own picture and became part of it while still being the artist.

---

[98] John 3:7 (ESV).
[99] John 14:8 (MSG).
[100] John 14:9 (MSG).
[101] Exodus 3:14 (ESV).
[102] John 8:58 (ESV).

Once again, you will find plenty of people telling you it is impossible for Jesus to be God and man. And it is very difficult to understand. Some, like the Jehovah's Witnesses, will argue from their version of the Bible[103] to say He was a created being. I cannot go into the arguments here. It would take too long. But if you want to read up on the Trinity, I wrote an ebook called *The Trinity*. It is available on Amazon. You can search in their search bar for 'Trinity Neil Laing' and you will find it, or look at the link in the reference below[104] for the UK version. It is also available on the US Amazon site.

If you want to know what God is like, look at Jesus. But we can't think of God in our normal terms – anything we can see or measure – so it wasn't Jesus' body that revealed God; it was no different from anyone else's body. It was His character; what He was like. As a man, He was totally obedient to God and so was able to do anything God wanted Him to do. Not only were people healed when He commanded but the winds and waves of the sea obeyed Him, too. Do you know anyone like that?

No religious leader I know of has ever been like Him. Muhammad performed not a single miracle. He said the Qur'an was the miracle. Some Old Testament prophets

---

[103] The Watchtower version (the New World Translation) is wrongly translated wherever the Bible disagrees with the Jehovah's Witnesses' ideas.

[104] https://www.amazon.co.uk/Trinity-Laying-Deep-Foundations-ebook/dp/B005MR4SX6/ref=sr_1_1?s=digital-text&ie=UTF8&qid=1508268353&sr=1-1&keywords=trinity+neil+laing (accessed 10th September 2017).

such as Moses, Elijah and Elisha did perform miracles, but none was like Jesus.

You may find it difficult to think that this man, Jesus, who lived 2,000 years ago was also God, but think about this. He lived for thirty-three years; He started as a carpenter working for His 'father'; He spent three years as an itinerant preacher; He never wrote a book; as far as we know, He never travelled outside His country of birth apart from when He was a very small child in Egypt; He never owned any real estate or had any riches; He was crucified by the Romans before He'd reached middle age. And yet, there is absolutely no one in the entire history of the human race who has had the influence on us that His life has had, and His influence is still as powerful as it always has been. How come?

You'll have to read the Bible to find out what this man who is God was like. I've lost count of how many times I've read it. And every time I read it I find out more. I get to know God more. It's the same with countless people. The Bible isn't a textbook. It brims with life and living. It's not a how-to manual, it's a be-like manual. I dare you to read it.

But God, we have a problem. Why do you allow so much suffering?

15. Why Would a Good God Allow Suffering?

When I was at school, I read C S Lewis' book about suffering called *The Problem of Pain*.[105] I can strongly recommend that you read it if this is something that genuinely bothers you. It bothers a lot of people and it's right that it does. It has caused lots of people to become atheists because they would say:

- If God is all-loving, He would want to stop all suffering.

- If He is all-powerful, He is able to stop all suffering.

- The fact that we see so much suffering, especially when so much is undeserved, means God is either not all-loving, or not all-powerful, or both.

- We can conclude, therefore, that an all-loving, all-powerful God does not exist.

---

[105] C S Lewis, *The Problem of Pain* (London: Harper Collins, 2012).

That seems like straightforward logic, and it is something we need to examine and answer seriously.

The animal world

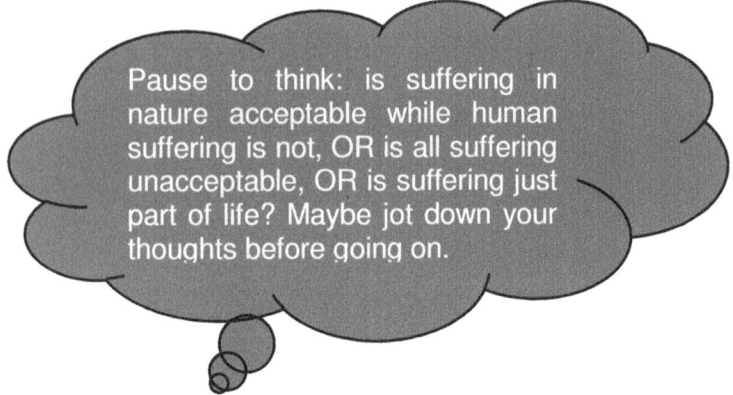

Pause to think: is suffering in nature acceptable while human suffering is not, OR is all suffering unacceptable, OR is suffering just part of life? Maybe jot down your thoughts before going on.

Suffering and death are very much part of the animal world. It would be lovely if no animal had to be killed to feed another – if every one of them was a herbivore. But having carnivores provides a means of maintaining a balance so that there are not too many herbivores to destroy the plants. The variety of organisms is vastly increased by having producers, primary, secondary, tertiary and more consumers.

Coming from Africa, I saw much of this suffering, especially as I wanted to be a game ranger. Very few animals in Africa die of old age. Virtually everything – even a lion – is killed by another animal, because if they get old, they are no longer able to protect themselves, and there is always something ready to kill them.

But human beings do die of old age; the vast majority are not killed by animals or other humans. Humans, however, experience forms of suffering no animal can know anything about. Animals do not tend to have psychological problems; young animals don't get nasty texts from others; they're not bullied on social media; they don't worry about their looks or whether they're too fat or thin. They're not under pressure to pass exams. They don't worry about what they will make of their lives. They do have a constant struggle to survive, however.

I don't find that many people have a huge problem with animals suffering in the wild though we are concerned about human cruelty to animals. But our big concern is why do people have to suffer so much?

Job – the man who suffered

There is a book in the Bible which has its central theme around the suffering of one man called Job (pronounced 'Jobe') who, totally undeserved, suffers in an appalling way.

It has forty-two chapters and books have been written about it so there's no way I can give you a learned interpretation, but I'll summarise it.

Job was a really godly man who always did what he felt was right. Satan (the devil) told God the only reason Job was so good was because God had helped him so much – he knew where his bread was buttered. God told the devil he could mess Job's life up as much as he wanted – apart from killing him – and he would see what Job would do.

The next moment Job lost everything – his wealth, his servants and all his children – all gone. He still trusted God but then he got hammered in his body. He came up in boils all over and all sorts of other ailments. I don't know how any of us would react, but he would not give up trusting

God. He did, however, start wishing he had never been born, and constantly asked God what he had done to deserve this, insisting he had done nothing wrong as far as he knew.

A bunch of 'friends' came to comfort him, but then tried to be helpful by saying he must have offended God and if he would just admit it, God would bless him again. Some Christians are like that, I have to admit. Anyway, the more he insisted he had done nothing wrong, the worse they reckoned he must have been. Nice friends!

In the end, God intervened and told the 'friends' they had got it wrong while Job hadn't. But He spoke almost roughly to Job as well and never told him why he had suffered. However, He then blessed Job with twice as much as he had before. But the most important thing is that Job came so much closer to God in the process, so, even though he had no textbook explanation, he somehow understood things in his heart. He said to God, 'I had heard of you by the hearing of the ear, but now my eye sees you.'[106]

Looking at the argument that an all-loving, all-powerful God cannot exist, we have to see that it is based on assuming that our view of suffering is the one that matters. But maybe God sees things from a different perspective – from an eternal one. Now, that may not be very satisfactory and it's also obvious, from the book of Job, that it is very difficult to give any sort of easy answer to this problem. But, perhaps our assumptions about God and suffering could be wrong.

---

[106] Job 42:5 (ESV).

Murder, barbarity and fruit

In 1978, in what was then Rhodesia, we had a friend, Wendy White, who was teaching at my old school, Eagle School, in the Vumba Mountains. Having closed, it had been taken over by the Elim Church and they had a mission school there. One night, a bunch of Robert Mugabe's terrorists arrived, herded all the missionaries out on to a playing field, raped all the women, including Wendy, and then hacked all of them, including their children – plus a three-week-old baby – to death with machetes in an unspeakable show of brutality.[107]

They had done nothing but attempt to give their lives to helping African children. The children and baby had done nothing at all. How could any of them deserve this horror? Unlike Job, they could learn nothing through it – they were all dead. The newspapers in the UK and in Rhodesia were understandably horrified and utterly condemned the atrocity. It really was horrific. But the Elim Church issued a statement saying they forgave the terrorists. Many people said that was stupid – when Jesus prayed on the cross, He had said, 'Father, forgive them; they don't know what they're doing.'[108] These men, people said, knew exactly what they were doing. They deserved no forgiveness. The fact is, though, that none of us deserves forgiveness, but amazingly God offers it to everyone on this earth. Forgiveness doesn't excuse the wrong; it just refuses to hold it against the wrongdoer.

---

[107] http://www.elim.org.uk/Publisher/File.aspx?ID=184349 (accessed 15th October 2017).
[108] Luke 23:34 (MSG).

We struggled to come to terms with it. How could human beings behave in such a depraved, barbaric and hateful way towards people who had done them absolutely no harm? The only word that came to me was when Jesus, speaking about how He would give His life for us, said, 'Truly, truly, I say to you, unless a grain of wheat falls into the earth and dies, it remains alone; but, if it dies, it bears much fruit.'[109]

Before Wendy died she had shown a strong faith in God, praying for forgiveness for their murderers even though she knew what was going to happen. So did a number of other missionaries there. Those terrorists had murdered and went on to murder other missionaries, and in each case were amazed at what they saw in them. As a result of the murder of the Elim missionaries, the schoolchildren were scattered among other mission schools and brought a new view of life with God the Holy Spirit to those missions.

Years ago, we heard that many terrorists involved in that atrocity were by then Christians, a number of them being church leaders. They realised the utter evil of what they had done, turned to God for forgiveness and had their lives completely transformed. They have, no doubt, affected many other lives. That would not have happened if that atrocity and others had not occurred. Some grains of wheat died but God brought about far more fruit from those deaths than would have been the case otherwise. The Elim Church was right to forgive.

---

[109] John 12:24 (ESV).

We have known suffering, with multiple deaths in our families in a short time, and with illness and pain, and there is no way I think there is an easy answer. In the space of about four years, we lost my father, my aunt, my wife's aunt, my brother, who died after a car accident, my wife's uncle, who committed suicide, and two weeks later, my wife's mother. Anyone who tries to give you a simple answer to this does not understand it. But those who have suffered are able to help others who are suffering in a real way.

Jesus suffered by crucifixion (a most horrible death) though He never did anything wrong in His life. He did it so that countless millions, like you and I, could find forgiveness for all they had done wrong. So, we know God knows all about suffering – He has gone through it. But He looks beyond it to something far better.

In the book of Hebrews, the author says we should 'run with endurance the race that is set before us, looking to Jesus, the founder and perfecter of our faith, who for the joy that was set before him endured the cross, despising the shame, and is seated at the right hand of the throne of God'.[110] Jesus clearly knew that His suffering was for a purpose, and so was able to go through this terrible, agonising death.

Can we blame God?

One other thing it is important to understand is that God gave us free will. We are not robots who have to obey Him. If we want to do the wrong thing, He lets us. We might

---

[110] Hebrews 12:1-2 (ESV).

think He should take away free will from those who are really nasty, but that would deny their humanity. And how nasty do you have to be before your free will is taken away? No one is perfect. I'm not; you're not. He could make us all into robots, but then we would not be made in His image at all. Would you want someone loving you because they are made to do so? That would not be love.

So, if some people cause human misery to others, we cannot blame God. We have turned away from Him and decided not to obey Him. The consequence is that we all suffer – whether we deserve it or not.

Another thing I have found is that generally people who have suffered in some way are much nicer people than those who have never suffered. Somehow, they seem to understand others better; they have more time for people. You feel you can talk to them more easily. I would not really want someone leading a church if they had not suffered. Jesus 'learned obedience through what he suffered'.[111] Maybe we all have something we can learn through suffering.

Suffering will continue to be a difficult question to deal with. And it is made doubly difficult if you have not experienced what I described in chapter 14 as being born again. Until then, you can only see it from a human perspective. That is why Jesus said, 'You must be born again.'[112]

---

[111] Hebrews 5:8 (ESV).
[112] John 3:7 (ESV).

Conclusion

I have said most of what I want to say to you already! So, let's sum up and see what we've learned and where we go from here.

Science is great

I don't know how much you enjoy science, but I can tell you it gets more interesting as you go on. It's not all about learning facts; it's about discovering things and understanding how things work. Much of what you learn at school is facts (things other people have discovered), and you need that before you can go on and discover things yourself. You need to understand how science works before you can work it.

Once you do, though, all sorts of possibilities will open up to you. You could be the person to discover the cure for HIV. How would that make you feel? Maybe you think that's true; maybe you think it's rubbish. That's up to you! In a way, it's to do with faith of a sort.

If you can get a scientific angle on the world and universe, it will help you to analyse things, look at them critically and decide more easily if something is true or not.

I think believing an explanation about something that is clearly scientific nonsense is stupid. Unfortunately, lots of religious people do that and, as a result, you can get some very weird ideas. Although this is highly unusual and hardly anyone believes it, I have actually met people who really think the earth is flat, that the sun and moon are only a few miles up in the sky and that Antarctica is a rim of ice around the edge of the world to stop the oceans falling off into space!

If you believe the universe is 6,000 years old, you are perfectly entitled to your opinion, but I would like to say, give me proper scientific evidence – evidence that can stand up to argument from other people who disagree and know what they're talking about. Believing in creationism does not mean you have faith. And deciding to believe the Bible does not necessarily mean you have faith.

Faith makes us more complete

There's no way science can give us everything, no matter how great it is. I've already discussed poetry with you. The same can be said for abstract art. We need to have a second angle on life to appreciate it. Faith helps you to look beyond the science (not to ignore it) to see what is behind all that we can see and measure.

I think of it rather like those 'magic eye' pictures. What is 'really' there is a pattern on paper; all sorts of shapes and so on. There isn't anything else at all. But if you look 'through' the picture by relaxing your eyes so that they try to focus behind the pattern, suddenly a 3-D picture emerges – usually something that has nothing to do with the pattern.

Is that 3-D picture actually there? No, it isn't but, in a way, it is. Because the pattern was designed specially to show that picture. That is the purpose of it. But it's just an image that is constructed in your brain.

Some people try to see the picture by looking directly at the pattern and imagining shapes, but that doesn't work. They think that people who can see the image are just imagining it. But they're not. You have to look beyond. If you do, you will see the same thing as everyone else sees.

That's like faith. From a scientific viewpoint, God isn't there. And I mean it – He isn't because He's not part of creation. But if you look beyond the science, the purpose of this creation begins to emerge. It will never work as long as you stick with just looking at the things we can see obviously. You must look beyond. Countless people have done so and found it works. And the amazing thing is they nearly all see the same sort of thing. That's faith. Remember what I said before. Just deciding to believe the Bible does not produce faith. Faith is a conviction of the heart; it's looking beyond the creation and 'seeing' the Creator.

Faith has no problem with science, as people seeing a magic eye picture have no problem with the pattern. But people with faith know that if they don't look beyond the science, they will never see the meaning behind it.

We need to accept each other

To me, this business of thinking science and faith are opposed to each other is a load of old do-dah. We need to be able to work together and appreciate each other. I am not saying a scientific outlook is essential for life, but let's appreciate the people who benefit humankind by working in science. And we can all have a healthier attitude that looks for evidence and refuses to believe stuff that has absolutely none.

But people who insist that anything that does not have experimental scientific proof is untrue are also being stupid. Life cannot continue like that. If you insist on only seeing life scientifically, you will be missing out on so much.

Scientifically, love does not exist, but our experience tells us that it does. We may be able to explain our emotions scientifically, but they are still our emotions. If I explain my love to my wife in scientific terms, I don't think she would be too impressed! A whole lot of what I experience may have some scientific basis, but it actually goes beyond science.

If you want to understand life in its wholeness, you need far more than science. I don't enjoy a rainbow because I understand the electromagnetic spectrum; I enjoy it because it is beautiful. And when I enjoy anything, I don't think about the release of enjoyment hormones such as endorphins in my body; I just enjoy it.

Science studies every process in the universe that has to do with matter, energy and so on, but it cannot look beyond the universe. However, it is completely illogical to say that this means there is nothing beyond the universe. Whatever theory you hold, the universe had to have some way of being there. Something had to start it and that something could not be part of the universe. Christians call that 'something' God.

Whether or not that 'something' is the same as the God the Bible describes is another matter, and different religions disagree over that, but there has to be *something*.

Carl Sagan wrote a book called *Pale Blue Dot* and said:

> How is it that hardly any major religion has looked at science and concluded, 'This is better than we thought! The Universe is much bigger than our prophets said, grander, more subtle, more elegant'? Instead they say, 'No, no, no! My god is a little god, and I want him to stay that way.' A religion, old or new, that stressed the magnificence of the Universe as revealed by modern science might be able to draw forth reserves of reverence and awe hardly tapped by the conventional faiths.[113]

Sagan is quite right about the science. Whether you like science or not, it can open your eyes to stupendously amazing things. And reverence and awe are what worship is about.

The unbelievably tiny, like electrons or quarks or quantum gravitational waves, to the unbelievably huge, like stars that make our sun look like a pinprick, and galaxies that are hundreds of thousands of light years across, to say nothing of the whole universe, is mind-boggling. When you look at such fantastically complex things as the inner workings of cells or the minute balance

---

[113] Carl Sagan, *Pale Blue Dot* (New York: Random House, 1994), quoted by: https://www.goodreads.com/quotes/48918-how-is-it-that-hardly-any-major-religion-has-looked (accessed 18th October 2017).

of all the systems of a living creature, you realise how staggering life is.

But the God of the Bible is most decidedly not a 'little god'. The Bible's God is infinitely greater than the universe. He designed and made it! The Bible tells me that appreciating what He has made (perhaps by studying science) enables me to understand more about Him. Science is not about God but, as a Christian, I can appreciate more and more of God through science if I accept that it has all come from His hand.

God isn't little or big. He is infinite and that's something else altogether. He's outside space and time, but also completely involved in it. The Bible gives me the poetry, if you like, that opens up a whole new view beyond the science. It's a view that never ends and, for me and for anyone who cares to explore it, it is constantly expanding.

If you think it's just about what you learn in RE or RS, or whatever your school calls it, then you haven't understood the tiniest bit of it. I'm not saying there is anything wrong with your RE, but it can't tell you what knowing God is really about.

Atheists are totally unaware of this extra dimension and so they think it can't exist. But the experience of millions of people is that it does and it's not just wishful thinking. The Church is not supposed to be a cosy club. It's where people can discover the wonder of life and living in the power of God.

Jesus came to sort out and get rid of the rubbish and bring people into life and light. He was no namby-pamby. Yes, He was loving, but He was also incredibly tough and He led a group of young men and women who went out and started changing the world. And that is still happening.

If you want to find out what life is all about, you need to look beyond your nose, beyond your life, beyond science. Just around the corner, a corner you may not be able to see right now, a whole different view is there to discover. You need to look around that corner.

I was taken by this quote from Robert Jastrow that I found on the web. He was director of the Mount Wilson Institute and co-founder of NASA's Goddard Institute. He wrote a book *God and the Astronomers* and, in it, he said:

> This is an exceedingly strange development, unexpected by all but the theologians. They have always accepted the word of the Bible: In the beginning God created heaven and earth … [But] for the scientist who has lived by his faith in the power of reason, the story ends like a bad dream. He has scaled the mountains of ignorance; he is about to conquer the highest peak; [and] as he pulls himself over the final rock, he is greeted by a band of theologians who have been sitting there for centuries.[114]

If you are a Christian who has to take everything in the Bible absolutely literally, I appeal to you to look beyond the words and see the spirit behind them. You also have a corner to turn; you can discover treasures in the Bible you

---

[114] Robert Jastrow, *God and the Astronomers* (New York: W W Norton and Co, 1992), p6., quoted by:
http://www.simpletoremember.com/articles/a/science-quotes/ (accessed 18th October 2017).

never thought were there; you can also discover treasures in science which do not contradict the Bible but can cause you to worship.

If you have thought, like so many, that science has the answers and there is no need for God, then maybe you need to do some more thinking and, like some top-notch scientists, admit that there is far more to life than you ever imagined was possible; that perhaps, out of sight in the background of all existence, is a God who created all things.

You may not have to climb the scientific mountain to discover Him; you may not have to work everything out to believe He is there. If you are humble enough, you can ask Him to show Himself to you. You could end up stepping around the corner and discovering Him – and, with Him, you'll discover real life.

Famous Scientists Who Are Christians

You may well have been led to believe that nearly all true scientists are atheists. Richard Dawkins seems to be of that opinion. It's probably true, if you look all over the world, that the majority are atheists, but the majority of people in the world are not Christians anyway. Jesus told us that most people do not find life,[115] so perhaps we shouldn't be surprised. As I said at the beginning, it's not decided by a vote or by who is most intelligent.

Scientists are half as likely to believe in a higher power as are the general public, according to a survey conducted by the Pew Research Center in 2009 in America.[116] Thirty-three per cent of scientists there say they believe in God and a further 18 per cent say they believe in a sort of universal spirit or higher power compared with 95 per cent of the general American public who believe in God or a higher power.

---

[115] Matthew 7:13-14.
[116] http://www.pewforum.org/2009/11/05/scientists-and-belief/ (accessed 20th October 2017).

In past centuries, in the West, science or natural philosophy was led to a great extent by scientists who were Christian believers,[117] such as Isaac Newton (who had the apple fall on his head), who called himself a Christian but was probably more a deist.[118] Johannes Kepler, who developed ideas on planetary motion, Galileo, who reckoned the earth was not the centre of the universe and believed in the non-literal interpretation of Scripture but was persecuted by the Roman Catholic Church, Sir Francis Bacon, Michael Faraday, Robert Boyle, Carl Linnaeus, Alessandro Volta, Charles Babbage, James Clerk Maxwell, Gregor Mendel, Lewis Carroll, Louis Pasteur and many others.[119]

In the last century, there are names such as Lord Kelvin, Marconi, Pierre Teilhard de Chardin, Max Planck, Georges Lemaître, Charles Coulson and Sir Robert Boyd among many others.

Those who are still living include Denis Alexander, director of the Faraday Institute for Science and Religion at the University of Cambridge, Francis Collins, director of the National Institutes of Health (appointed by President Obama) – he was the former director of the US National Human Genome Research Institute – Keith Fox, professor of biochemistry at Southampton University, Alister

---

[117] Don't confuse 'Christian Science', which is a religious cult, with true scientists who are Christians.

[118] A deist is someone who believes there is some sort of God but that He is impersonal, that He designed the universe and its laws and then left it to run on its own.

[119] https://en.wikipedia.org/wiki/List_of_Christians_in_science_and_technology (accessed 20th October 2017).

McGrath, who holds a DPhil in molecular biophysics and a doctorate in divinity, both from the University of Oxford, Gerhard Ertl, a Roman Catholic and winner of the 2007 Nobel Prize in Chemistry, William D Phillips, winner of the 1997 Nobel Prize in Physics and one of the founding members of the International Society for Science and Religion, John Lennox, who is emeritus professor of mathematics at the University of Oxford, John Polkinghorne, who was professor of mathematical physics at the University of Cambridge and is now an Anglican priest, and I could go on and on![120]

There are hundreds of top-notch scientists who have seen beyond the science and realised there is more to life than their science, that it is not the only way to understand the universe. They feel that faith gives them a better view by seeing life and the universe from two different angles.

Some of these people have been atheists and have come to the point of realising they had misunderstood what Christian belief is about and have become believers.

Some examples include Allan Sandage, an astronomer who explored the wonder of the universe[121] and became a believer. Another slightly different example is Antony Flew, an atheist who spent much of his life attacking

---

[120] https://en.wikipedia.org/wiki/List_of_Christians_in_science_and_technology (accessed 20th October 2017).
[121] http://www.washingtonpost.com/wp-srv/newsweek/science_of_god/scienceofgod.htm (accessed 20th October 2017).

religion. He did not become a Christian, but a deist – someone who believes in a remote higher power.[122]

Francis Collins, whom I mentioned above, is another one who was an atheist,[123] and Alister McGrath made that journey, too.[124]

Another interesting one is an astrophysicist, Sarah Salviander, who grew up an atheist but became convinced that the God of the Bible is true.[125]

Dr Sylvia McLain writes in *The Guardian* that the idea that all scientists are atheists is rubbish.[126]

I strongly recommend you look some of these references up and check them out.

---

[122] https://strangenotions.com/flew/ (accessed 20th October 2017).

[123] https://www.premierchristianity.com/Blog/How-a-world-famous-geneticist-went-from-staunch-atheist-to-Christian-convert (accessed 20th October 2017).

[124] https://jamesbishopblog.com/2015/05/18/former-atheist-alister-mcgrath-becomes-a-christian-because-of-science/ (accessed 20th October 2017).

[125] https://jamesbishopblog.com/2015/05/23/former-atheist-astrophysicist-sarah-salviander-explains-her-journey-to-christianity/ (accessed 20th October 2017).

[126] https://www.theguardian.com/science/occams-corner/2013/mar/04/myth-scientists-religion-hating-atheists (accessed 20th October 2017).

Top Ten Questions Asked by Teenagers

1. Does evolution take away the need for God?
I hope I have answered this one. Evolution is the best theory we have for the origin of life and the variety of organisms on earth, based on pretty firm evidence. It is an explanation for how it all came about. Saying God created all things is a statement, not an explanation. It says God is responsible for all of creation – not only in the beginning, but continually. We don't need God as an explanation, but that doesn't mean He is unnecessary. We do need Him to give life meaning. The theory of evolution and natural selection tells us the mechanism God put in place to make organisms able to adapt to constantly changing conditions. A friend of mine described it as the 'software of creation'.

2. Is there a limit to the science God wants us to do?
God gave us our intelligence, our ability to investigate and our enquiring minds. I believe He fully intends us to use them and is glorified when we do what He designed us to do. In making us after His image, He made us as creative beings and creativity is not only to do with art; it means inventiveness and using our imaginations to contribute to

society. So, no, there is no limit to the science He wants us to do.

3. Why doesn't God come and live on earth and keep order?

Firstly, He has come to live on earth when He came in Christ. He came as a man, just like us; if that man lived physically on earth forever, He would not be like us. He has given us His Spirit to enable us to live His way. But He wants us to respond freely to Him. If He forced order on earth, we would not be able to respond to Him freely.

4. Will science ultimately take over religion as humanity continues to develop?

In some ways, yes, I think it will. It will take over all religion that is based on no evidence and on superstition. However, that is not what God wants of us. He wants a personal relationship with us rather than us following religious rituals which mean nothing. Science and faith are not opposed to each other, so I would say we need more and more of each. Science should enhance our faith, and faith make us appreciate science more.

5. Is there scientific evidence for God?

As God is not part of the universe, science cannot investigate Him, but it can investigate things like miracles which are used as evidence for God. However, none of that can be used as direct evidence for God, so there is no direct scientific evidence for God, but there is plenty of evidence that points to a belief in God being perfectly reasonable, provided you understand what we mean by God.

6. If God really cares and is all-powerful, why does He allow suffering to happen?

I discussed this in chapter 15 on suffering. It is a very difficult subject on which to give a simple answer. But we tend to want answers purely from our point of view rather than seeing the bigger picture of what God achieves in our lives as a result of suffering. We also have to see that we are free to rebel against Him as well as to love Him. So, if someone causes suffering to others, we can blame that person, not God. God could intervene but He would stop us being free in the process.

7. How do you interpret Genesis in light of the Big Bang?

There is no conflict between Genesis and the Big Bang if you accept that the days in Genesis may not mean twenty-four hours. Genesis says there was a beginning; according to the Big Bang theory, there was a beginning. Other Bible passages speak of God stretching out the heavens, which is a poetic description of the continually expanding universe.

8. Do you ever question your religion because of what you learn in science?

Yes, I do. If I think something conflicts with what I believe, I will question what I believe. That especially happened when I first became a Christian and I didn't understand the relationship between science and faith so well. However, the more I get to know God, the more I realise there is no conflict, so I know there is an answer even when I may not have it.

9. Why did God choose to create the earth?

As I am not God, I can't answer that one completely. However, it seems to me, He delights in creation. He loves His creation – every bit of it – and so He created a whole universe. The earth is especially suited to sustain life and He wanted to make a wonderful variety. He also wanted to create a particular creature He could have a close relationship with – actually billions of these creatures – each a special individual – you and me – who would be something like Him. We could then enjoy this beautiful creation together with Him. He seems to be a God who delights in sharing.

10. Does science allow for miracles?

The amazing thing about nature is that it is ordered and that was what made early scientists feel that nature was evidence for God. However, if God set up the laws by which nature works, He is also able to suspend them temporarily or make them work differently from normal if He wants to. I think that with any miracle, something highly unusual happens, but that it comes within some scientific process. I don't think God violates His own laws. So, in some sense, science should allow for miracles, even though we may not understand them. To say miracles cannot happen because we can't understand them seems to me to be bad science.

Further Reading if You Want More

Here are a few more links for you to follow if you would like to explore faith in God and science a bit more.

5 Reasons Why Science and Faith Are Compatible:
https://cccdiscover.com/5-reasons-why-science-and-faith-are-compatible/

BuzzFeed: We Asked 12 Scientists How Their Faith Affects Their Work:
https://www.buzzfeed.com/kellyoakes/scientists-and-faith?utm_term=.njpqD88YAx#.jq0p5009rQ

Evidence for Jesus' resurrection by someone who set out to disprove it:
Frank Morison, *Who Moved the Stone?* (Milton Keynes: Authentic Media, 2006)

Tackling the problem of suffering:
C S Lewis, *The Problem of Pain* (London: Harper Collins, 2012)

Science Has Found Proof of the Existence of God (title of YouTube video):
https://www.youtube.com/watch?v=Er9D00DXQQs

Theistic Evolution Organisations and Resources

Affiliation of Christian Geologists:
www2.wheaton.edu/ACG/

Answers in Creation (Old Earth Ministries):
www.oldearth.org

Christians in Science: www.cis.org.uk

BioLogos: https://biologos.org

Genesis Proclaimed Association:
www.genesisproclaimed.org

God and the Big Bang: https://gatbb.co.uk/

Interdisciplinary Biblical Research Institute: www.ibri.org

Perspectives on Theistic Evolution:
www.theisticevolution.org

Reasons to Believe: www.reasons.org/

Solid Rock Lectures: http://solidrocklectures.org

The American Scientific Affiliation (ASA):
http://network.asa3.org

The Faraday Institute for Science and Religion:
www.faraday.st-edmunds.cam.ac.uk

The Science and Religion Forum: http://srforum.org/

Bibliography

Alexander, Denis, *Creation or Evolution: Do We Have to Choose?* (Oxford: Monarch, 2008).

Dawkins, Richard, *The God Delusion* (Random House eBooks, 2009).

Hitchens, Christopher, *God Is Not Great* (London: Atlantic Books, 2008).

Jastrow, Robert, *God and the Astronomers* (New York: W W Norton & Co, 1992).

Koenig, Harold G, McCullough, Michael E & Larson, David B, *Handbook of Religion and Health* (Oxford: Oxford University Press, 2001).

Laing, Neil, *Even Dawkins Has a God* (Bloomington, IN: WestBow Press, 2014).

Marshall, Catherine, *Beyond Ourselves* (London: Hodder & Stoughton, 1962).

Sagan, Carl, *Pale Blue Dot* (New York: Random House, 1994).

Sims, Andrew, *Is Faith Delusion?* (London: Continuum, 2009).

Twain, Mark, *Following the Equator*, Public Domain ebook).